JP.

BRITISH AND IRISH ANCESTORS

FAMILY HISTORY FROM PEN & SWORD

TRACING YOUR BRITISH AND IRISH ANCESTORS

A Guide for Family Historians

Jonathan Scott

Pen & Sword

FAMILY HISTORY

First published in Great Britain in 2016
PEN & SWORD FAMILY HISTORY
an imprint of
Pen & Sword Books Ltd
47 Church Street,
Barnsley
South Yorkshire,
S70 2AS

ISBN 978 147385 325 6

A CIP catalogue record for this book is
available from the British Library.

Typeset in Palatino by CHIC GRAPHICS

Printed and bound in England by
CPI Group (UK), Croydon, CR0 4YY

Pen & Sword Books Ltd incorporates the imprints of Pen & Sword
Archaeology, Atlas, Aviation, Battleground, Discovery, Family History,
History, Maritime, Military, Naval, Politics, Railways, Select, Social History,
Transport, True Crime, Claymore Press, Frontline Books, Leo Cooper,
Praetorian Press, Remember When, Seaforth Publishing and Wharncliffe.

For a c | LANCASHIRE COUNTY | act
47 Churcl | LIBRARY | igland

CONTENTS

'But it'll leave us practically penniless!'
For Genevieve

Chapter 1

BEGINNINGS

WHAT YOU KNOW

Imagine this: you've just woken up and found yourself alone, on top of a hill. You stand up. You have no idea where you are or how you got there. Let's throw in some fog. There, it's foggy. You need to get home, but to do that you need to figure out where you are. What do you do first? You look around.

Family history, to begin with, is much the same. You start by taking a look around. You need to check the ground beneath your feet, to check what you're standing on is firm. You need to remove any assumptions, you need to try and forget everything you think you know and concentrate on facts. And very slowly, like a person with arms outstretched feeling their way through a foggy landscape, you move from the known into the unknown, checking your footing with every step.

Pennie, Penrose, Kate, Warren. Just some of the names my mother goes by.

Take your mother's first name. Most of you will assume you know your mother's first name. But do you actually know it? Do you have her name recorded on a birth certificate nestled away in your family archive? Can you lay your hands on irreversible proof that the name you have just jotted down is the same as the name that the state holds?

If you had met me just fifteen years ago and asked me my mother's first name, the answer I would have given you would have been wrong. Indeed, the answer she would give you today would not be the same as the answer the state would give. I was in my twenties by the time I finally picked up a letter and asked: 'Why does your bank always call you Kate?' I was expecting a tale of misunderstanding never put right, but it turned out her name is Kate. It was the name she was born with, baptised with and registered with, just not the name she ever went by. And this is more common than you might think. People often don't go by the names they were given. I went to school with a boy who veered between calling himself Simon (his middle name) and Piers (his first name).

'I can trace my family back to 1066 don't you know!' The author as irritating youth.

When you enter the first antechamber of genealogical research you not only need be aware of what you don't yet know, but also *what you think you already know.* It may sound unimportant, but checking birth, marriage and death indexes is the first chore for many a researcher, and it's amazing just how many family historians are almost immediately thwarted – often because of erroneous assumptions and family myths. As an irritating, corduroyed youth, I would boast to anyone who would listen that I could trace my family back to 1066. In the words of my former editor Simon Fowler, that turned out to be 'rubbish'. (He actually used a different word.)

Now, this book is aimed at researchers from all over the world tracing British and Irish roots, the emphasis being toward readers who can't easily travel here to conduct research first hand. That's not to say I will ignore physical sources that have to be checked in person – far from it – but the focus will predominantly be on sources, services, finding aids and advice that can be found online.

Getting Started

Go to wherever you keep your old stuff and take it out. If you don't have any kind of family archive, don't worry, just skip to the next chapter. But if you do, dive in, lay it all over a carpeted floor while a radio plays something you like, and organise it into categories. Your categories could be Immediate Family (if you find the short-form birth certificate of your mother, put this here), Wider Family (a named photograph of a great uncle in his service uniform would be put here), Unknown (for any unnamed photographs/items) and Miscellaneous (for random ephemera such as ancient bills or uniform buttons).

Now start drawing up a very rough family tree, with all the names of members of your immediate family, then spreading out to the next generation. To begin with I'd suggest drawing this up free hand, but you can of course print out all kinds of blank trees from the Internet if you prefer, or go straight to your computer and enter the details there.

Write down all the birth, marriage and death dates that you think you know. I suggest a colour code: black for certainties, pencil for virtual certainties that you need to double check and red for blind assumptions.

In the next section I go into a little more detail about the process of interviewing family members, but in general I'd advise that you remain suspicious of memories, including your own. Humans are excellent at combining memories, stealing other people's and incorporating them into their own, and distorting time. Family legends are like that. My grandfather could certainly claim an association with legendary flying ace Douglas Bader (they both worked for Shell), but I suspect sometimes that the stories were expanded.

In short: don't assume and watch out.

Right from the start you will need to be sensitive. There may be secrets just beneath the surface of your family's party line.

Some may benefit from an airing, others might not be ready to come out.

Now there are lots of books that concentrate on first steps, so I'm not going to spend too long repeating the tips and cliches, but I will end this section by suggesting some of my favourite on and offline sources. In general I find the writing of genealogical scribes Kathy Chater, Chris Paton, Simon Fowler, John Grenham, Anthony Adolph and Nick Barratt friendly, clear and easy to follow, and all focus on British-centric resources in the main. They each have strengths too – Chris is a font of knowledge on all things Scottish, John is the man for Irish research.

ONLINE RESOURCES

FamilySearch, Getting Started:
  familysearch.org/ask/gettingstarted
ScotlandsPeople > Help & Resources > Getting Started:
  scotlandspeople.gov.uk
Federation of Family History Societies, Really Useful Leaflet:
  ffhs.org.uk/really_useful_leaflet.pdf
Free UK Genealogy: freeukgenealogy.org.uk
FamilySearch, Research Forms:
  familysearch.org/learn/wiki/en/Research_Forms
FamilyTree, Getting Started: family-tree.co.uk/getting-started/
Genuki: genuki.org.uk/gs/
Society of Genealogists, Getting Started: sog.org.uk/learn/help-getting-started-with-genealogy/
Cyndi's List, Getting Started: cyndislist.com/free-stuff/getting-started/
Ancestry, Getting Started: ancestry.co.uk/cs/uk/gettingstarted
British Genealogy Network: britishgenealogy.net
PRONI, Getting Started:
  www.proni.gov.uk/index/family_history/family_history_getting_started.htm

FURTHER READING

Adolph, Anthony. *Collins Tracing Your Family History,* Collins, 2008

Barratt, Nick. *Who Do You Think You Are? Encyclopedia of Genealogy*, Harper, 2008

Chater, Kathy. *How to Trace Your Family Tree*, Lorenz Books, 2013

Fowler, Simon. *Family History: Digging Deeper*, The History Press, 2012

Waddell, Dan. *Who Do You Think You Are?: The Genealogy Handbook*, BBC Books, 2014

CHARTING YOUR FAMILY

All you need to begin with is a large piece of paper and a pencil. Websites, software and mobile apps will be clamouring for you to enter names and dates into their online family trees. This is a great option, but I would wait until you have your immediate family and perhaps one generation back nailed before going digital.

You've already gathered together what documentary evidence and photographs exist in your family archives – certificates, diaries, letters and photographs. Alongside your large piece of paper, you should arm yourself with an A5 reporter's notebook or an A4 legal pad (or some method of digital note taking). And this is the most important thing to remember: *start writing everything down.*

Keeping notes becomes increasingly important as you delve further into an individual's life, so you need to start out as you mean to carry on. If you hear from aunt so-and-so that great uncle so-and-so played first-class cricket for Glamorgan in 1948, then write down the fact and where/when it came from. The most frustrating thing about family history is when you do a little digging, then life takes over and you don't touch your research

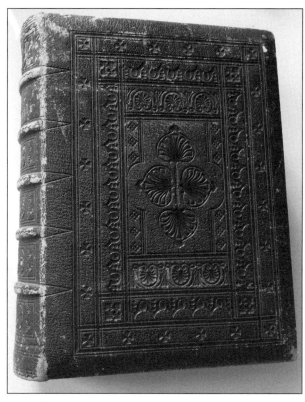

Family bibles can be excellent sources of information, often including detailed family trees. This Victorian example has Family Register pages sandwiched between the Old and New Testaments.

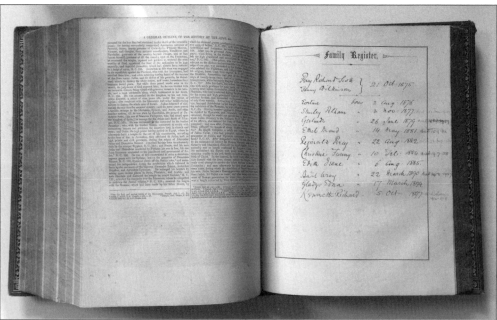

for a month or two, and before you know it, you're spending an afternoon re-treading the same path.

You need to be in the habit of noting not only the facts/information you gather, but also where you gathered them from – your sources. Just as importantly you need to note down not only the searches that lead to fruitful information, but also those that turn up nothing. The only thing more annoying than a blind alley, is a blind alley you've been down before.

Now many starting out guides include tips that say the likes of 'check whether anyone has already researched your tree'. I've never quite understood this, as it seems like such a double-edged sword. Yes, it will save you work, but you're only saving yourself from the very thing you're setting out to do. It's like setting out on a marathon, only to decide that as all these other people are running it you don't need to.

That said, if someone's been there before it will of course save you much of the tedious early leg-work, meaning you can concentrate on the more 'fun' aspects of genealogy. But, at the same time, fixing names and dates of individuals is a vital learning curve that everyone needs to go through. So, even if you do find yourself presented with a fairly complete family tree, I'd still suggest you go back to the sources and double-check names and dates for yourself.

Assuming you have some names and dates, notes on other information such as military service or occupation, plus some notes/reminders concerning any family stories or anecdotes that you want to check, it's time to begin the family interviews.

If you're in close contact with relatives and can begin your interviews with relative ease, I recommend getting to it, but taking a belt and braces approach – some kind of simple audio recorder plus a notebook. If you live miles or continents away from your nearest and dearest, then some email or handwritten correspondence will be called for. Make sure, however, that if you go for this latter method that you are specific about the questions you want answered. It's easy to sound vague when writing an email requesting information, and vague questions will lead to vague answers. Many genealogists start out by drawing up a simple questionnaire, or printing out a ready made template of questions from websites such as FamilySearch, and as jumping off points these function very well.

When talking to relatives an open and flexible approach is best. You need to be flexible in terms of timings, but also in terms of what you are ready and willing to hear. The individual may not wish to talk about what you want to ask about. Listening carefully, taking time, will all help you get the most out of your interviewees.

When I started out as a local reporter, one of my many bad habits was the habit of excitedly jumping in with my own story during an interview. This, I soon realised, was a derailing thing to do. It can often blow conversations off course. By all means chip in, but you need to hold yourself back, to try not to interrupt and to listen. Everyone thinks they are good listeners, including me, but it's an underrated skill that takes effort. Imagine you're nearest and dearest is talking to you, while you're watching television. Yes, you may be able to repeat back everything they have just said, but they won't *feel* listened to. To listen, and to show that you're listening, you need to give eye contact, you need to repeat back what you've heard to check you're understanding. In other words, you need to pull the conversation, rather than push.

If you're using recording devices (which I would recommend), you need to be up front. Make it clear that you will be recording what they say, and check this is alright with the interviewee. If it's not, put it away and take notes. You will have to wait for them to settle into the conversation. Knowing one is being recorded, or just having someone making notes as you speak, can be an unsettling experience at first. You need to give people time to get used to it.

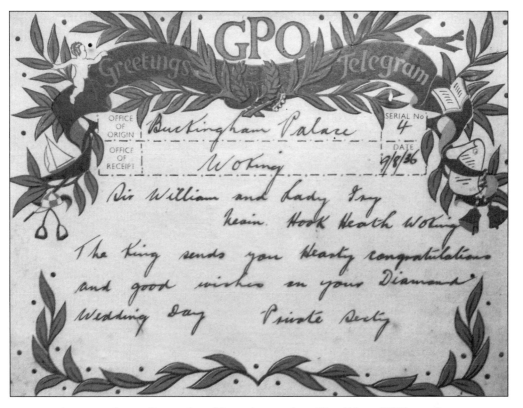

A congratulatory diamond wedding telegram from King Edward VIII, sent just months before his abdication.

You may go there determined to fix a date, but you also need to be open to what is being said. You may want to be specific, but giving space may lead to valuable but unexpected information. You need a spectrum of questions that range from the specific to the more general: from the 'where were you born?' to the 'what do you remember about ____?'

Memories are imperfect. People's perception of time can be particularly troublesome – an incident from two years ago can seem like a decade ago, an incident from decades before, can seem like yesterday. Memories can bunch together, can disguise themselves, can lie. So, you need to take everything with a pinch of salt. That's not to say you should be cynical and doubting, but simply that you must take a rigorous approach to sifting what information comes in, to sort out what is known, and what remains hazy, what's hearsay and what needs to be checked.

Families come complete with skeletons, secrets, scandals, rifts, divides, jealousies and neuroses. When you start out on your mission to find out more, just be aware of the feelings of your family. If you encounter resistance, respect the resistance and give it time.

During these interviews, you may be shown, or might ask to see, pieces of documentary evidence. You will need to write down the most important information contained within, and describe exactly where it comes from. You could also ask permission to borrow or copy the items. Again, if you bring along a camera, have a tablet computer or smartphone, you can quickly and easily take a perfectly serviceable copy right then and there. But again, be sensitive. People may be unwilling or uneasy about having precious photographs or items relating to loved ones out of their hands, or even copied.

Another decision to make at this early stage is your research goal. Do you intend to just go back as far as you can? Or perhaps there's a particular family legend you wish to investigate. Having an achievable and manageable goal will help give shape and direction to your research. Many start by concentrating on a particular branch of the family, while others might choose just one period of one person's life – such as an individual's wartime service career.

REMEMBER
- Work from what you know.
- Fix and confirm dates of birth, marriage and death, then work backwards.
- If you're starting out and have several branches of the family to choose from, opt for the branch with the rarer surname. A less common surname makes your work much easier – great when you're learning the ropes.
- Talk to relatives. Watch out for any nicknames and name changes. Ask to see any photos, letters or documents.
- If possible record your interviews.
- Take too many notes. You just never know what will come in useful when. So take a thorough approach and note everything down.
- Have a manageable goal. Perhaps choose a branch of the family or an individual to focus on.
- Check if anyone else is researching your family – you could at this point sign up to the likes of MyHeritage or GenesReunited, which can help you find researchers with shared interests.
- Focus on identifying when and where a person lived. Most records generated about a person will be associated with a place.

ONLINE RESOURCES
About.com, 50 Questions to Ask Your Relatives:
genealogy.about. com/cs/oralhistory/a/interview.htm

FamilySearch, Creating oral histories:
familysearch.org/learn/wiki/en/Creating_Oral_Histories

Oral History Society: www.ohs.org.uk

THE STATE AND THE PARISH

My intention in this section is to arm you with a rough and ready guide to the way the parish, county and state function together. I won't bog you down with lots of information you don't need, but a working knowledge of local government and ecclesiastical administration and boundaries will help you find records, interpret those records and predict possible pitfalls before they happen. If you're on an expensive research trip to some county record office, it would be rather frustrating to learn that the parish material you seek is in the diocesan record office 50 miles away, or that the parish you thought was in one county, turns out to share its name with the small chapelry in a neighbouring county.

There are differences in the structure of local government across the constituent parts of the UK partly because they each derive from systems in place prior to unification. It wasn't until the population explosion of the Industrial Revolution that some systems of local government were reformed, modernised and partially unified.

If you read nothing else in this book, simply hold on to this piece of advice: spend some time confirming the location of your ancestor's home parish, and then confirm the location of records relating to that parish. If you're at all familiar with military research, you will know that 'the unit' is the basic currency – know the unit in which an individual served and this gives you the keys to the city. Similarly, with much genealogical research, the parish is the vital thing to know.

Local expertise is invaluable. There are many regional quirks and inconstancies, with shifting boundaries of parish, hundred, diocese and county, coupled with further confusion over types of boundary (ecclesiastical, civil, poor law, etc.), which can unsettle researchers new to an area. This is where the network of county family history societies, each with their own pools of expertise, can really come into their own.

Administrative Divisions

First let's go top-down through the basic administrative divisions: Country/State/Parliament > County/Shire > Borough/District > Hundred > Parish. Meanwhile, in England, ecclesiastical units can be summarised: Church of England > Province (Canterbury and York) > Archdiocese > Diocese/bishopric > Parish.

The Anglo-Saxon Kingdom of England was divided into 'shires' – the shire being the traditional term for a division of land. Today those shires are known as counties – which is why so many British counties have 'shire' within their county names.

A nineteenth-century map of Kent. Traditionally if you're born east of the River Medway you're a 'Man of Kent', west of the river, you're a 'Kentish Man'. Happily I was born in Surrey.

The shire, or county, was further divided into 'hundreds', also known in some areas as wapentakes or wards. Indeed, until the introduction of districts by the Local Government Act 1894, hundreds were the only widely used descriptive unit between the parish and the county. Hundred boundaries can be logical and neatly aligned in ways you would expect, but they are often independent of both parish and county boundaries – in other words a hundred could be split between counties, or a parish could be split between hundreds. Over time, the principal functions of the hundred became the administration of law and the keeping of the peace – so there would be hundred courts held every few weeks to tackle local disputes or crimes. But the importance of hundred courts gradually declined, most powers shifting to county courts when these were formerly established in 1867.

Over the centuries there was a gradual administrative split between town and country. Henry II and other monarchs granted royal charters to many towns across England (which were thereafter referred to as boroughs). For an annual rent to the Crown, the towns earned themselves privileges such as the exemption from feudal payments, rights to hold markets and to levy certain taxes. In other words they paid for the rights to make money and have a modicum of self-government.

In the 1540s the office of Lord Lieutenant was instituted in each county, becoming the Crown's direct representative in a county and also responsible for raising and organising the county militia. Local justices of the peace took on various administrative functions, presiding over roads and institutions and could levy local local taxes. If borough status gave towns specific rights, so wannabe cities could lobby for greater independence from the county, effectively becoming their own state, with their own set of officials, powers and quarter sessions courts.

The ecclesiastical parish is the jurisdictional unit that governs Church affairs within its boundaries, each keeping its own records. Small villages will often be part of a larger parish, the 'headquarters' of which are elsewhere. And a parish may consist of one or more chapelries, dependent district churches or 'chapels of ease' – a chapel situated closer to communities that lived a long distance from the parish church.

In contrast to an ecclesiastical parish, the civil parish is the lowest tier of local government (below districts and counties). Today a civil parish can range in size from a large town with a population of around 80,000 to a single village with fewer than a hundred inhabitants. Civil parishes in their modern sense were established by the Local Government Act 1894, when parishes were grouped into districts and each civil parish had an elected civil parish council.

A misspelling can lead researchers down blind alleys. This portrait has a rough family tree inscribed on the reverse. However, the parish of Joseph Smith is noted as Ashton Flauville, when it should be Aston Flamville.

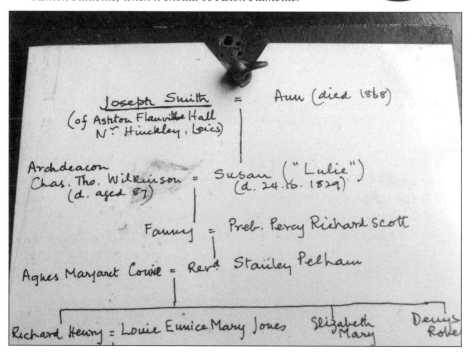

These divisions and boundaries cause most trouble when you actually set out to find a particular record. Let's look at Yorkshire. Changes in 1974 transferred some North Riding parishes to County Durham, while Harrogate, Ripon and the Skipton area, all previously in the West Riding, formed part of the newly created county of North Yorkshire. Records for the part of North Yorkshire that was formerly part of the East Riding are held by the East Riding Archive Service in Beverley. Meanwhile, North Riding archives still hold records relating to the parts of the former North Riding lost to Durham and Cleveland/Teesside under the boundary changes of 1974. Therefore, a genealogist new to this particular area would need to find out whether their ancestor's records are likely to be held at North Yorkshire County Record Office in Northallerton, Teesside Archives in Middlesbrough, Durham County Record Office or at the Borthwick Institute at York University.

There are also complications caused by ecclesiastical jurisdiction. The western portion of North Yorkshire is in the Archdeaconry of Richmond and formerly in the diocese of Chester. So wills before 1858 and Bishop's Transcripts for that area are held at West Yorkshire Archives at Sheepscar, Leeds. The eastern side of North Yorkshire is in the Archdeaconry of Cleveland, and so early wills and the Bishop's Transcripts are at the Borthwick Institute.

Scotland and Ireland

In Scotland the equivalent to the borough was the 'burgh', the first royal burghs dating from the twelfth-century reign of King David I. These burghs enjoyed some autonomous freedom, including rights to impose tolls and fines on traders within a region. The oldest document held at the Aberdeen City and Aberdeenshire Archives is a Charter of King William the Lion of *c.* 1190, which grants the Burgh of Aberdeen the right to its own merchant guild, confirming an earlier charter of his grandfather King David I. Aberdeen's Town

House Charter Room holds – among other things – the city's charters and deeds, as well as burial registers, guildry records and the minutes of the council from 1398 to the present day – the oldest council minutes in Scotland.

The origins of Scottish counties lie in the sheriffdoms over which local sheriffs exercised jurisdiction. After the Acts of Union 1707 burghs continued to be the principal sub-division of Scotland. Then after reorganisation in 1889 local administrative units comprised counties > cities > large burghs > small burghs. Meanwhile, congregations of the Church of Scotland and other Presbyterian churches were governed and administered by the Kirk Session, which consisted of elected members and a minister.

Irish land divisions can seem equally complicated. Broadly they run as follows, province > county > barony > parish > townland.

Modern-day Ireland is split into the Republic of Ireland and Northern Ireland. Across the whole island there are four provinces, each divided into counties. The Republic of Ireland comprises the provinces of Connaught, Leinster and Munster, and three counties within the province of Ulster (Cavan, Donegal and Monaghan). Then Northern Ireland, which is part of the UK, consists of the remaining six counties of the province of Ulster (Antrim, Armagh, Derry, Down, Fermanagh and Tyrone).

These four provinces are the oldest sub-divisions and broadly follow ancient clan kingdoms, but no longer hold an important administrative purpose. More important is the barony. While baronies were made obsolete in 1898, they were used to describe different areas in many important genealogical sources such as land surveys. Annoyingly, these baronies often span parts of multiple civil parishes and counties.

Today counties are more important administratively, and each has a county town/city, and each is divided into civil parishes. As with the UK, there are two types of parish: ecclesiastical and civil. Finally, each civil parish is divided further into townlands (not to be confused with towns). The townland is the smallest official division, originally based on an area deemed sufficient to sustain a cow.

Ecclesiastical parishes are further complicated because there are both Church of Ireland parishes and Roman Catholic parishes, which again have different congregations and boundaries. The Irish Genealogy Toolkit offers a really good guide to this complicated situation (www.irish-genealogy-toolkit.com/Irish-land-divisions.html).

Finally, all over the UK and Ireland there were administrative divisions of Poor Law unions, which were established during the nineteenth century to tackle increasing poverty. We will look at these in more detail in Chapter 4, 'Secrets, Scandals and Hard Times'.

If you're reading this and feeling overwhelmed, please understand that is not my intention. I want to illustrate that things are complicated, but I'd also want to reassure you that there is a lot of guidance and expertise out there. Genuki (genuki.org.uk), for example, has in-depth guides to civil and ecclesiastical parish boundaries in counties across the UK and Ireland. Indeed, while it's not the most modern website to look at, its greatest strength is its simplicity. It is a very good place to get to grips with the local administration and records of an area.

REMEMBER
- Shire: a traditional term for a large division of land, which is why so many counties have 'shire' within their names.
- Ecclesiastical parish: the parish is the jurisdictional unit that governs Church affairs within its boundaries, each keeping its own records. Small villages will often be part of a larger parish, the headquarters of which are elsewhere. A parish may consist of one or more chapelries, dependent district churches or 'chapels of ease' – a chapel situated closer to communities that lived a long distance from the parish church.

- Chapelry: a small parochial division of a large, populated parish. Most would keep their own parish registers of baptisms and burials, and where authorisation was granted, marriages could be performed and registers kept. In particular, Lancashire, Yorkshire, Cheshire and Greater London have many parishes divided into many more chapelries. The largest parish in England is the one served by Manchester Cathedral – within its bounds there are over 150 smaller chapels.
- Diocese: parishes grouped together under the jurisdiction of a bishop. Some dioceses include one or more archdeaconries administered by an archdeacon.
- Parish records: 'parish records' usually means parish registers. 'Parish chest' records are other parish-level sources such as settlement examinations, removal orders, apprenticeship indentures and more.
- The United Kingdom Census of 1911 noted that 8,322 parishes in England and Wales were not identical for civil and ecclesiastical purposes.
- The 'Danelaw counties' of Yorkshire, Derbyshire, Leicestershire, Northamptonshire, Nottinghamshire, Rutland and Lincolnshire were divided into 'wapentakes' instead of hundreds. 'Danelaw' refers to parts of England where the laws of the Danes held sway.
- Deanery: a group of parishes forming a district within an archdeaconry.
- In Wales traditional and now largely obsolete units of land division include cantref/cantred or commote.
- Electoral district: a territorial sub-division for electing local Members of Parliament. It is also known as a constituency, riding, ward, division, electoral area or electorate.
- Catholic parish boundaries are different to those of the Church of England.

> **ONLINE RESOURCES**
> Genuki: genuki.org.uk
> Irish Genealogy Toolkit, Irish Land Divisions: www.irish-genealogy-toolkit.com/Irish-land-divisions.html
> ScotlandsPeople: scotlandspeople.gov.uk

> **FURTHER READING**
> Cox, J. Charles. *Parish Registers of England*, Methuen, 1910
> Humphery-Smith, Cecil R. *The Phillimore Atlas and Index of Parish Registers*, Phillimore, 2002

ARCHIVES IN BRITAIN AND IRELAND

You cannot beat the excitement of actually visiting an archive in person and handling a document that contains a reference to, or even the handwriting of, your ancestor. To this end there is a network of national and regional archives across the UK and Ireland, many of which can boast documents stretching back to the Middle Ages. Hull's archives include a document from 1299, while one of the oldest items held at the London Metropolitan Archives dates from 1067 – a charter from William the Conqueror sent to the city just after the Battle of Hastings, but before he entered London. It's basically a message of reassurance, an eleventh-century 'keep calm and carry on', a promise, written in English, that he wasn't about to trash the place.

There are many hundreds of archives across the British Isles. First, there are the national collections: the National Archives of Scotland, The National Archives in Kew (TNA), the British Library, the National Library of Wales, the National Library of Scotland, the National Archives of Ireland, the National Library of Ireland and the Public Record Office of Northern Ireland (PRONI). Next, there is a network of county level archives, and

The National Archives' 'Find an archive' page allows you to search for archives, museums and other repositories across the UK. Scroll down and you can also explore overseas archives by country.

below these borough or city collections, museum collections, university special library collections, specialist libraries and local history libraries.

Assuming you know when and where a member of the family lived, your first port of call should be the relevant county or borough archive. Thankfully, for those who cannot easily visit in person, we are living through a period of mass digitisation, meaning more and more can be achieved remotely from simple catalogue or index searches to downloading images of original documents. In this respect some counties across the UK have gone further than others. Some record office websites boast digitised sources and helpful finding aids, others are still some way behind. Some have struck longstanding agreements with the likes of Ancestry, FamilySearch, TheGenealogist and Findmypast, others have not started down this road. So, if you are researching in what appears to be something of a digital backwater, and can't visit the archives in person, you may need to look into research services the record office or local family history society can offer, or think about hiring a professional.

Most archives' collections include county, borough, town, parish and other local government records, parish chest material, electoral registers, tax records, photographic collections, local newspapers, records of institutions such as hospitals and schools, court material, records of individuals, families and charities. They will normally offer banks of microfilm/fiche readers and lines of computers, usually providing free online access to commercial websites such as Ancestry and sometimes to internal digital finding aids.

Alongside the 'usual' sources, there will be collections unique to the area – local business records, or collections relating to individuals. The Surrey History Centre in Woking, for example, has the family papers of Lewis Carroll, author of *Alice's Adventures in Wonderland*, garden plans, watercolours and photographs by Gertrude Jekyll, the Robert Barclay collection of Surrey illustrations and the Philip Bradley Collection of fairground photographs. It also has the diaries of English antiquary William Bray, which features what is believed to be the earliest known manuscript reference to baseball. On the day after Easter in 1755, the then 18-year-old William wrote: 'After Dinner Went to Miss Seale's to play at Base Ball, with her, the 3 Miss Whiteheads, Miss Billinghurst, Miss Molly Flutter, Mr. Chandler, Mr. Ford, H. Parsons & Jolly. Drank tea and stayed till 8.'

Alongside county archives, there may be city, borough or town collections. These sometimes form part of one unified county service, or are administered separately. The ancient boundary lines of the county of Essex covered parts of what is now Greater

Most local history libraries maintain collections of local newspapers. When searching any source you should always have spelling variants in mind. This local newspaper story calls my mother 'Penrose Warner', instead of Warren. And they don't even bother to name the dog.

BEST-LOOKING PAIR IN THE SHOW

Penrose Warner, nine, of Hook Heath, Surrey, and her three-month-old dachshund, won first prize for the " best-looking owner and dog " at a show organised by the Mayford branch of the Woking Conservative Association.

London – namely the modern London boroughs of Newham, Redbridge, Havering, Waltham Forest, Barking and Dagenham. Today each of these maintains its own borough archive so researchers with interests here may find relevant material in both the Essex county collections and the local borough collections.

Many libraries across the UK have local studies departments. These can make an excellent alternative to the county archive as a research venue as they often offer microform access to county wide collections (such as parish registers or census material), and usually offer free online access to the likes of Ancestry and Findmypast. Local studies collections can also include original manuscript collections such as newspapers, photographs, electoral registers and more.

Finally, hundreds of museums pepper the British Isles, and many maintain their own archival collections. Some will be preserved on site, others may have been deposited with the county archive. Many will have very basic websites, with little more than details of how to visit, others will have searchable catalogues, digital photo libraries, research and look-up services, digitised databases, indexes and more.

The place to start your search for an archive used to be known as Archon, but is now simply the 'Find an archive' service through TNA's Discovery catalogue (discovery.nationalarchives. gov.uk/ find-an-archive). This allows you to browse archives in England, Northern Ireland, Scotland and Wales, or conduct separate searches for overseas repositories. You can search by area or by name of the archive. A search by 'mining' returns seven results, including the National Coal Mining Museum for England, the Mining Records Office and the Scottish Mining Museum. For archives in Ireland you can use the Irish Archives Resource (www.iar.ie), an online database that contains searchable archival descriptions.

Using Catalogues

Assuming most of your research concentrates in one area, it is likely you will quickly become familiar with the county's archival catalogue. Most, but not all, are online. Some have their own dedicated catalogue website, others are only available through larger multi-archive catalogues such as Archives Wales or TNA's Discovery (which has records from TNA and over 2,500 archives across the UK).

It's important to understand how much a catalogue can reveal.

An online catalogue is a searchable database of the documents and books held by the repository. These are finding aids, designed to help you find relevant documents and note down references so you can then request to view the documents in the research/ reading room.

The amount of information contained within county catalogues varies a great deal – not only from archive to archive, but also from collection to collection within the same archive. Some name-rich sources popular with genealogists will often have been name indexed so they are more easily searchable. But many will not. Some searches may result in simply the name or title of an uncatalogued collection. In addition, you may find that not all collections are available for public consultation.

More sophisticated catalogues will link direct to images of the original documents and photographs. Most catalogues will include thousands of names, without necessarily functioning as a full index to all documents. So, you might be able to search the catalogue for details of the church records they hold, but you won't be able to trawl by all the names that appear in the baptism, marriage or burial registers.

Most will give descriptions of each item including the following fields: a reference or finding number, a title and date, and some detail about the parent collection. So, you search the catalogue, find an item of interest, then use the reference or finding number to order the item in the research room – many archives have online request forms. (They may also offer copying or look-up services for remote researchers.)

The Essex Record Office catalogue Seax (seax.essexcc.gov.uk) is a good example. It boasts indexes and many free images of documents, as well as links through to ERO's own subscription service, Essex Ancestors, where you can download images of parish registers and wills for a fee.

Online catalogues offer various advanced search options to help narrow your field. Sticking with Seax, it offers an 'Advanced

Mode' option where you can search for different words or phrases by filling in the fields on screen. So, if wish to locate an electoral register for a certain year, you type 'electoral register' into one field, the name of the parish in another, then fill in the date field and click search. You can also use catalogue references to narrow searches within certain collections: type 'Chelmsford' in the first field and 'SA' in the second and it will search all references to Chelmsford within the Sound Archive.

Always be wary of narrowing your search too quickly. If you narrow by a parish that turns out later to be incorrect, you may miss the vital reference you have been searching for. Also most catalogues offer some kind of browse option, where you simply click on different categories or collections. This is often a good starting point as it is likely to reveal background information, giving each collection its historical context and explaining the kind of documents that have survived.

Some important multi-archive catalogues include: TNA, Discovery (discovery.nationalarchives.gov.uk), Archives Wales (archiveswales.org.uk) and the Scottish Archive Network (scan.org.uk).

Researching From Abroad

Another potential source of help and advice can be genealogy discussion groups, which often cover specific regions, time periods, surnames and more. Genuki maintains a database of mailing lists and newsgroups at (www.genuki.org.uk/indexes/MailingLists.html). There are also the vast networks of message boards (Ancestry's are at boards.ancestry.com), which include specialised topics such as surnames and locales. At the time of writing there were 25 million posts on more than 198,000 boards. Commercial genealogical websites normally offer some kind of 'community' or social networking features, which allow you to get in touch with other family historians working in the same area or researching the same surname or branch of a family.

Dedicated online forums can also be an excellent platform for posing queries, or finding out more about what the wider digital community is up to in your area of research. Just reading other queries and replies from other researchers can often resolve your own problem before you even have to ask it.

Rootschat is one of the largest UK forums (rootschat.com), with thriving specialist sections and threads, including many sections aimed at beginners and an archived library of threads going back to 2003. Other general interest examples include GenForum (genforum.genealogy.com), LostCousins (forums.lc/genealogy/index.php), British Genealogy & Family History Forums (british-genealogy.com) and Family History UK Genealogy Forums (forum.familyhistory.uk.com). Specialist examples include the Family Tree DNA (forums.familytreedna.com/), the Great War Forum (1914-1918.invisionzone.com/forums/), the British Medal Forum (britishmedalforum.com) and the regional Birmingham History Forum (birminghamhistory.co.uk/forum/).

Hiring a Professional
If you catch the genealogy bug, only to find that you simply don't have the time or resources to invest in a dedicated research trip, it might be time to hire a professional.

Many county record offices, regimental museums and genealogical societies offer various look-up services. These can be specific to a source – such as parish material perhaps – or a more generalised research service, with a sliding scale of charges. Most also offer copying services, where for a fee they will supply digital or paper copies of specific documents or entries. This can be a convenient way of remotely accessing records that have not yet been digitised.

If you are researching from overseas and need more help, hiring an expert on the ground can save both time and money. You might choose to hire a professional for advice, or to use a particular skill or specialism, or simply to carry out the more time-consuming legwork. You might ask them to research your entire family, one branch of the family or a single individual.

Having selected a professional, you need to approach them with all the relevant details of your research – what is known and what is unproved – and then explain what you want, which questions you want answered. As with hiring a mechanic to fix your car, you need to find out if the researcher can help, what it will cost, how long it will be before they can start and when they expect to complete the project.

Many professionals charge on a basis of an hourly rate, which, according to a useful Society of Genealogists' guide on the subject, varies from £20 to £50 per hour ('and perhaps more or less'). The same guide urges you to bear in mind the different types of researcher – those whose work is their sole source of income, and those who see it as a secondary activity. Remember though that many researchers will not be able to give an accurate estimate of cost until they have begun, as some tasks may prove more time-consuming than expected. Most professional genealogists usually ask for money in advance and once the work is complete the resulting reports should include pedigrees, typed up transcriptions, copies and details of everything that was searched – including all the sources where nothing useful was found.

Some record office websites have lists of recommended professionals, which can be a good option as they are likely to have local expertise. Otherwise you can browse advertisements on websites and in magazines, search via genealogical forums or Twitter, or go through professional associations such as the Association of Genealogists and Researchers in Archives (www.agra.org.uk).

REMEMBER

To find an archive:
discovery.nationalarchives.gov.u
archiveswales.org.uk
scan.org.uk
www.iar.ie

To find a genealogical group:
Federation of Family History Societies: ffhs.org.uk
Scottish Association of Family History Societies: safhs.org.uk
Guild of One-Name Studies: one-name.org

To find a professional researcher:
The Association of Genealogists and Researchers in Archives:
    www.agra.org.uk
The Association of Scottish Genealogists and Researchers in
    Archives: www.asgra.co.uk
The Society of Genealogists: www.sog.org.uk
Includes a useful 'hints and tips' guide to hiring a professional.
The Association of Professional Genealogists in Ireland:
    www.apgi.ie
Institute of Heraldic & Genealogical Studies: ihgs.ac.uk

FURTHER READING

Clarke, Tristram. *Tracing Your Scottish Ancestors*, Birlinn, 2012
Evans, Beryl. *Tracing Your Welsh Ancestors*, Pen & Sword, 2015
Grenham, John. *Tracing Your Irish Ancestors*, Gill & Macmillan,
    2012
Waddell, Dan. *Who Do You Think You Are?: The Genealogy
    Handbook*, BBC Books, 2014

Chapter 2

BUILDING BLOCKS: NATIONAL RECORDS

CIVIL REGISTRATION

When you start researching an individual, your first step should be to fix their date of birth, marriage or death in the civil registration records. This collection of records is the most significant genealogical resource of the modern era, which, in England and Wales, stretches right back to the start of Queen Victoria's reign. And thankfully a great deal of civil registration research can be carried out online.

You should by now have a piece of paper with some as yet unconfirmed names and dates. Now you need to find those names in the UK's state records of births, marriages and deaths, and hopefully get hold of copies (physical or digital) of the certificates themselves.

I will not spend too long on the mechanics of civil registration, but a little knowledge of how the system hangs together will help you understand how the records were created, and help you think your way around any unexpected problems that arise.

How Civil Registration Worked

Before 1837 only churches recorded births, marriages and deaths in England and Wales. Parliament had realised that a more accurate picture of the population was required not least for the purposes of taxation and defence. The legislation was passed and civil registration in England and Wales began on 1 July 1837.

Just as the basic unit of ecclesiastical record keeping is the parish, so the important basis of civil registration is the registration district. These districts were based on the Poor Law unions drawn up three years earlier. The district was divided into sub-districts, each with a Registrar of Births and Deaths, and every quarter the superintendent registrars would send copies of their district's registrations to the Registrar General in London. The registration districts hold the original birth and death records, and the General Register Office (GRO) holds copies. When the system began there were twenty-seven registration districts in England and Wales, but there was a reorganisation in 1852 which saw that number increase to thirty-three.

Births and deaths were the responsibility of the local registrar. The job entailed travelling through the district to record all births within six weeks of arrival and deaths within five days of departure. The registrars were motivated as they were paid per registration, but there was resistance to the system, and individuals were missed from both official birth and death records from this period. (If your ancestor appears to be missing it's worth going straight to contemporary parish records – of which more in the next chapter.) However, more robust laws introduced in 1874 made it compulsory to report births and deaths, and there was a system of fines imposed for any late registration.

While the registrar dealt with births and deaths, clergy of the Church of England were automatically entitled to perform and register marriages. Clergy of other denominations could not perform legally valid marriages until 1898 (from when they could apply to become 'Authorised Persons'). Prior to that date a Registrar of Marriages had to be present. Although civil marriages could be performed in the register office, these were very rare until the twentieth century.

There were two marriage registers that had to be completed and signed by the parties. When a register was full, one copy would be sent to the Superintendent Registrar and the other was

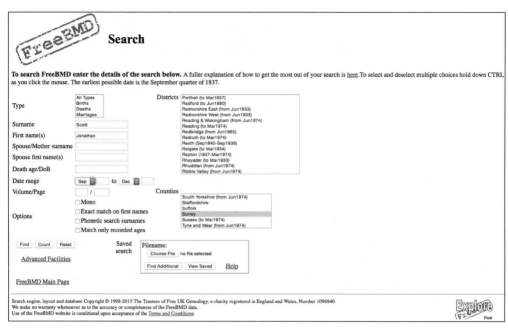

The FreeBMD website is an excellent place to start your search. Its aim is to provide a complete transcription and combined index to civil registration data.

kept at the church. In addition, quarterly copies of all marriages were sent to the register office and forwarded to the Registrar General. Quaker and Jewish marriages were performed by Registering Officers and Secretaries of Synagogues, respectively. They were also required to deposit completed registers at the register office, and to forward quarterly copies to the Registrar General.

Events were recorded on certificates – one copy retained by the registrar, the other given to whoever was supplying the information. Aside from any certificates that might survive in your family archive, the data should exist in two places – the original records held at the local level, and the copies held centrally.

Using Civil Registration Indexes

As registrations came in, alphabetical indexes were compiled on a quarterly basis. It is these quarterly indexes that are often the very first source the budding family historian will check – and when they find a hit they order a copy of the data retained in the GRO. This is why new family historians are often advised, if they have a choice, to choose the branch of their family that has the more uncommon surname. Just have a think about searching through every 'Smith' born in three months, as opposed to every 'McQuillan'.

These civil registration indexes are generally referred to as the GRO indexes. This name comes from the government department (the GRO) responsible for them. There are various on and offline sources where you can begin to search the GRO indexes for England and Wales – from regional indexes produced by local register services or genealogical groups to nationwide indexes through pay-per-view or commercial bodies.

As it is free, useful and available to all I am briefly going to concentrate on FreeBMD. FreeBMD.org.uk is an ongoing project to transcribe the civil registration indexes of births, marriages and deaths for England and Wales, and to provide free access to the transcribed records. It is part of the Free UK Genealogy family of websites, which also offers transcribed data from parish registers and census material. The transcribing is carried out by teams of volunteers and contains index information for the period 1837–1983. While incomplete, you can explore a regional breakdown of progress by event and year. Early in March 2016 the site contained 253,123,910 distinct records from a total of 323,007,107.

As has already been noted, GRO indexes were created alphabetically by quarters. The most useful aspect of this online project is that it represents the first consolidated master index. In addition, the original indexes were often only accessible on microform formats, and the quality of reproduction could often be very poor.

You enter your ancestor's surname, first name(s) and choose to search birth, marriage or death indexes. If you have a common surname, you will certainly need to have to hand additional search criteria to help you narrow your search: such as year of event, registration district, etc. Wildcards and multiple selections can also be used: such as selecting several registration districts simultaneously. Returned search results include the following information: event, quarter and year; surname; first name(s);

FONTMELL MAGNA WEDDING

Married at St. Andrew's Church, Fontmell Magna, on Saturday, were Mr. John Baliol Scott, 23, Ansdell Terrace,

London, W.8., eldest son of Mr. and Mrs. R. H. Scott, Old Chiswell Hall, Edenbridge, Kent, and Miss Penrose Warren daughter of Mr. and Mrs. Pelham Warren, Penn Hill Cottage, Bedchester, Shaftesbury.

The Rev. Bruce Shorten and Group Captain the Rev. Denis Coote officiated and the organist was Mr. Mark Venning (friend

This newspaper wedding report gives lots of details of the families of the bride and groom, useful for tracking down correct registration districts.

registration district; volume number; page number. Plus you will notice that the website also offers the ability, in many case, to see scanned images of the original index pages.

In general, the more parameters you specify the more precise the results will be, but remember that if you narrow results too far, and are using some piece of information that turns out to be incorrect, the more likely you are to miss the individual you are looking for. For example, if a relation consistently lied about their age, and you choose to search solely within that narrow date field, you will miss their entry. So you may well need to perform several searches. Remember too to try spelling variants – the website's own help page uses the example of 'Ian' – often spelt 'Iain'. Again, if you narrow by a name that is incorrectly spelt, you may miss the results containing your individual.

Another thing to keep in mind is that the quarter refers to the date the event was registered, not the date it occurred. Births were frequently registered late, so someone born at the end of June is likely to appear in the September quarter, or even later. Take particular care with specifying the district or county because it may not be what you expect. There's even more potential for confusion within densely populated areas like Birmingham.

Also information present in the records varies with year because the GRO only started adding data like date of birth, mother's maiden name and spouse name later in the creation of the index. So, searching for information that is not present will not return results, for example doing a search of births that includes the mother's maiden name will not return any records prior to September 1911.

Ordering Certificates: What They Can Tell You

Once you do have a match and you are confident that the match is the correct person you seek, you can look into ordering a copy of the certificate. You can order certificates either from the GRO (gro.gov.uk) or the local register office relevant to the certificate.

Even if you don't manage to find an index reference number in FreeBMD or any other source, you can still request a copy online provided you have sufficient information to identify the entry. You will need to supply the date of event, if you have it. If not, you enter 01/01/YYYY and staff search the specified year and one year either side. Ordering full certificates with or without GRO index reference supplied costs £9.25 – although without takes longer.

Full birth certificates include the name, date and place of birth, the father's name (if given at the time of registration), his place of birth and occupation, and mother's name, place of birth, maiden surname and (after 1984) occupation. The name and maiden name can help you track down the mother's parents, and from the September quarter of 1911 the mother's maiden name is included in the GRO index.

Marriage certificates contain the date and place of the marriage, the name, age and marital status/condition of the parties, the occupation and address. Most helpfully they also record name and occupation of each party's father, the name of the witnesses and the name of the person who solemnised the marriage. In this way they potentially arm you with information to begin your journey back along two branches of the family.

Death certificates are not quite as useful as they tend to just record details of the deceased: name, date and place of death, date and place of place of birth (before 1969 a certificate only showed age of deceased), occupation, address, cause of death and the name of the person who provided the information.

Civil Registration in Scotland and Ireland

Civil registration in Scotland started later, but it was also more detailed (although some details recorded at launch were soon dropped). Registers were kept from 1 January 1855, replacing registration by parishes of the Church of Scotland. From this date all registration was compulsory, regardless of religious denomination. And civil registration indexes for Scotland, which are separate from those of England and Wales, have been available for some time (on a pay-per-view basis) via Scotlands People.

Alongside what might be termed the usual information (name, sex, date, etc.), Scottish birth registers recorded place and time of birth, parents' names (including maiden name), father's occupation, name of informant and relationship to child, date and place of marriage. At launch even more details were included: in 1855 there was information on siblings and the ages and birthplaces of both parents, as well as their usual residence and date and place of their marriage.

Meanwhile, marriages included the date and place of marriage, name and occupation of both fathers, the name and maiden name of both mothers. Finally, death certificates included spouse's name, parents' names, occupations and whether they were deceased, cause of death, duration of last illness, doctor's name and details of the informant.

Copies, together with a full index, are available through ScotlandsPeople. The digital images on the site are scans of microfiche copies of the original register page. It therefore contains the same information you would normally see when looking at the actual record. Remember that birth records less than 100 years old, marriage records less than 75 years old and death records less than 50 years old are deemed 'modern day records' and so you will need to order an 'extract'. Extracts are certified, legally admissible copies of the specific register entry. Extracts of these records (as well as parish and census material) can be ordered from the site (£12 per extract).

Registration began in Ireland in 1864 (although registration of Protestant marriages had begun earlier in 1845). Again, registration districts were set up using boundaries of Poor Law unions. To take marriage as an example the certificates tend to include marriage date, place and denomination, names of bride and groom, their ages (frequently given as 'full age' – meaning of legal age), occupations, marital statuses, residences at the time of marriage, names and occupations of their fathers, and sometimes whether their fathers were deceased (this is not consistent), and signatures of the bride, groom and witnesses.

Unlike Scotland, there are a number of places to look for Irish registrations. For all of Ireland, the General Register Office in Roscommon has records of births, deaths (both 1864–1921) and marriages (1845–1921), and for the Republic of Ireland from 1921 to present. For Northern Ireland (the counties of Antrim, Armagh, Derry, Down, Fermanagh and Tyrone only) the General Register Office for Northern Ireland has records of births, deaths (both 1864 onwards), adoptions (1931 onwards) and marriages (1845 for non-Roman Catholic marriages, all marriages from 1864).

You can also access some civil registration data via pay-as-you-go or subscription at Ancestry, Findmypast and rootsireland.ie, and in addition there are index-only databases to civil records available for free via familysearch.org or irishgenealogy.ie. The latter's online indexes contain quite a lot of information – births after 1900, for example, include child's name, district/registration area, birth date and mother's maiden name.

You can order a photocopy of an entry in any register from the General Register Office or purchase an official certificate via certificates.ie (although again, remember that death records before 1924 and marriage records before 1903 are not currently available online). A certificate of an entry in any register, regardless of the year, can be purchased from the General Register Office using an application form.

REMEMBER

- Civil registration began at different times in different parts of the UK and Ireland: England and Wales (1837), Scotland (1855), Ireland (1864).
- Remember that English/Welsh birth registrations made before 1969 do not include details of the parents' place of birth and mother's occupation.
- If a father's name is missing from a birth certificate it may mean that the baby was illegitimate. Also, before 1875 a woman could name any man as the father without providing evidence. If there's a line through the name column, it means no name was given at the time of registration.
- The March quarter contains registrations in January, February and March. The June quarter contains registrations in April, May and June. The September quarter contains registrations in July, August and September. The December quarter contains registrations in October, November and December.
- Civil registration began in Ireland in 1864. However, registration of Protestant marriages had begun earlier in 1845.
- English and Welsh civil registration data is also available via commercial/pay-per-view websites such as Ancestry, Findmypast and TheGenealogist.
- TNA has various collections of births, marriages and deaths that were registered overseas – including British subjects onboard ships and those on military service. You can search these via specialist website BMDRegisters.co.uk or TheGenealogist.co.uk. Many pre-date the start of civil registration.
- The quarter refers to the date the event was registered not the date it occurred. Births in particular were often registered late. Someone born at the end of September is likely to appear in the December quarter.

- You can find out about researching Ireland's civil records in person, charges and ordering online at www.welfare.ie/en/Pages/General-Register-Office.aspx. The equivalent page for Northern Ireland is at www.nidirect.gov.uk/index/information-and-services/government-citizens-and-rights/order-life-event-certificates.htm.
- Before you start, you need to know the person's name (and if possible the names of closest family too), the approximate date of the life event and the district where the event is likely to have taken place.
- When searching indexes, try multiple spelling variations and keep shifting back and forward in time.
- If you cannot find a birth, marriage, or death record in civil registration, search church records.
- You can order certificates either from the GRO or from the relevant local register office.
- At launch, Scottish death certificates even recorded the name of the undertaker and when the doctor last saw the deceased alive, although these details were soon dropped.
- You can order copies of birth, death or marriage certificates from the GRO website (gov.uk/order-copy-birth-death-marriage-certificate). You will need to register and certificates currently cost £9.25.
- For Scottish research you can order official via nrscotland.gov.uk/registration/how-to-order-an-official-extract-from-the-registers, and for events in Northern Ireland from www.nidirect.gov.uk/index/do-it-online/government-citizens-and-rights-online/order-a-birth-adoption-death-marriage-or-civil-partnership-certificate.htm.

ONLINE RESOURCES

ScotlandsPeople: scotlandspeople.gov.uk

FreeBMD: freebmd.org.uk

UK BMD: ukbmd.org.uk/local_bmd

Links to county websites offering online transcribed indexes to original GRO records held by the local register offices.

GRO Certificate Ordering Service (England and Wales): gro.gov.uk

FamilySearch: familysearch.org

Has the likes of this England and Wales Death Registration Index (1837–2007) courtesy of Findmypast.

BMDIndex: BMDindex.co.uk

Camdex: camdex.org

Example of a regional facility, this one covering Cambridgeshire.

National Records of Scotland: nrscotland.gov.uk/research/guides/birth-death-and-marriage-records/statutory-registers-of-births-deaths-and-marriages

Irish Genealogy: irishgenealogy.ie

Scotland BDM Exchange: sctbdm.com

FURTHER READING

Barratt, Nick. *Who Do You Think You Are? Encyclopedia of Genealogy*, Harper, 2008

Osborn, Helen. *Genealogy: Essential Research Methods*, Robert Hale, 2012

THE CENSUS

The level of interest and coverage generated by the launch of the 1901 census took some in the genealogical world by surprise back in the early 2000s. It was perhaps the first mass release of an important totally new nationwide database since the more widespread uptake of the Internet during the later 1990s, and facilitated an explosion of interest in genealogical research. The 1901 census was where an entire generation of budding researchers started their journey.

Census returns open doors to all kinds of avenues of research. They allow you to find out or confirm simple facts about an individual – such as occupation, age and family, relationships and living arrangements – but they also assist you in making all kinds of deductions about a person's status, offer a portrait of the household and can give you a picture of the wider community. Assuming you can find your family in each set of census returns, they give you a decade by decade snapshot of their lives. They can also offer vital information to help you track down any civil registration records of births, marriages and deaths that have so far eluded capture.

The Pre-census Census

A census is a statistical count of the population of a country. Before and after the establishment of a country wide census system, there are types of records that can function as a kind of proto-census, compiled for a variety of reasons, often at a local level and often relating to property or systems of taxation. The Domesday Book itself can be viewed as a country wide stock take and early census (you can explore names recorded in the survey via opendomesday.org/name/). Or there are the Protestation Returns of 1642, when by order of the House of Commons all adult men were asked to swear an oath of allegiance to the Protestant religion. Aberdeenshire's county and city archives boasts the Aberdeen Poll Book of 1696, from a national poll tax that existed between 1693 and 1699. It was levied on individuals (rather than property) and payments were graduated in accordance with the taxpayers' financial status.

You may also find unique census-like sources that were compiled at the local level. West Glamorgan Archive Service, for example, preserves the 1837 and 1839 Town Surveys of Swansea.

These were originally planned and carried out by a local scholarly body that would eventually found Wales' first museum and become the Royal Institution of South Wales. Like the census, these surveys were organised by household and record the surname, occupier, proprietor, description of the property, rental/rateable value and address. The more detailed 1839 survey includes details of profession and/or business, the number of families/individuals at each property and their religion.

Other sources that can function as a census of an area include electoral rolls and militia lists. The latter were lists of able-bodied men suitable for service, and so provided a very rough census of men in a particular area. One example, again from the collections of Aberdeen City and Aberdeenshire Archives, are the lists of men who joined the 4th Regiment of Aberdeenshire Militia in 1809, at the height of the Napoleonic Wars, which record not only their names but also the men's complexion, hair and eye colour, profession (usually 'labourer') and their home parish and county.

In Ireland, in particular, you will often come across the term 'census substitutes' as so much of Ireland's original census material has not survived. The most famous of these is the Griffith's Valuation, a full-scale valuation of property in Ireland overseen by Richard Griffith and published in 1847 and 1864. It remains one of the most important genealogical sources for research into nineteenth-century Ireland.

A more recent census substitute, which can help researchers navigate the census desert of the 1930s and 1940s, is the 1939 Register, taken on 29 September 1939 and used to produce up-to-date population statistics, identification cards and later ration cards.

How the System Developed Over Time
The census system begins at the start of the nineteenth century, but becomes genealogically useful from 1841. A census has been taken every ten years since 1801, with the exception of 1941, and as the years went by the system became more exhaustive.

Early nineteenth-century censuses are little more than headcounts. So, the second census of Great Britain, for example, was taken on Monday, 27 May 1811. The returns gave a population of 12.6 million people (an increase of 1.6 million over 1801) and it recorded details such as the number of inhabited houses in a district, or how many persons in total – and how many male/female inhabitants. Details or names of individuals were not recorded in the census returns.

It was the 1841 census that was the first to list the names of every individual within the household. So when genealogists refer to the census, they generally mean records from 1841 onwards.

Although there were tweaks to what was recorded, the system remained largely unchanged through most of the nineteenth century. From 1841 to 1901, a schedule was completed for each household, which was then collected by the enumerator, who copied the information into enumeration books. It is these books that form the basis of what is now available to explore on and offline.

In 1911 all the household schedules were kept and these survive today at TNA. This time the schedules were not copied into enumeration books, instead the enumerators produced so-called summary books. These listed every address, including unoccupied buildings, and only contain the names of the head of each household.

What the Census Can Tell You

In 1841 the census forms recorded the first name/surname, age (but rounded down to the nearest five for those aged 15 or over), sex and occupation. There was also a yes or no answer to whether an individual was born in the county in which they were enumerated, and whether they were born in Scotland, Ireland or 'Foreign Parts'.

In censuses between 1851 and 1901, individual details included full name (often just initials for the middle name),

There's nothing more infuriating than an unnamed photograph. Thankfully this early example has both names and a date. We can also see that the print was framed in Jersey, which might be useful for finding the family in the census.

relationship to the 'head of the household' – usually the oldest male – marital status, age, sex, occupation, county and parish of birth, country of birth (if born outside England and Wales), whether they suffered from certain medical disabilities, the full address and information about the dwelling itself. Special enumeration books were completed for institutions such as workhouses, barracks and hospitals, and there were special schedules for vessels from 1851 onwards.

The 1911 census also recorded a married woman's 'fertility in marriage' – length of present marriage and number of children born of that marriage, living or deceased, more comprehensive occupational data, extra detail on nationality and the exact birthplaces for people born in Scotland or Ireland.

There are lots of reasons why an individual might appear to be missing from the census. Common reasons why you may not find someone in the data is simply through confusion over names. Many individuals might have given a different surname to the one you were expecting, perhaps because of re-marriage. People weren't always entirely truthful or accurate. A petty criminal might give a false name, an unmarried couple might want to appear married, while a separated couple might prefer to describe themselves as widowed out of sheer embarrassment.

Some individuals, especially in prisons, are only listed by name. Others might have adopted an unfamiliar short form or variation of their first name, or started favouring their middle name. Some people simply made themselves absent on census night – many suffragettes famously boycotted the 1911 census, for example. Another common reason to be missing from the headcount was simply being out of the country – working overseas or on active service with the army or navy.

However, more frustrating for researchers are the times when your ancestor is not missing, but the relevant bit of the census is. There are missing pages from all censuses, although the 1861 has suffered most in this regard. As Audrey Collins writes in her TNA blog article on this subject: 'The missing parts even of this census still only represent a tiny proportion of the whole census, but that still amounts to an awful lot of people.'

If you can't find someone in one online census index, try another. Indexes come from different projects and teams, so a transcription mistake in one may have been avoided in another. Even without an index, if you think you know where an ancestor was living, you can of course go straight to that address in the census. And if you are failing to find an individual make sure you have tried all the spelling variations (also taking into account potential transcriptions errors).

Where to Find It
Every census for England and Wales has been indexed. This page of the FamilySearch wiki (familysearch.org/learn/wiki/en/

England_Census) focuses on the census of England, but you can easily navigate to equivalent pages for other parts of the UK and Ireland. The site has a complete free index and transcription of the 1881 census, as well as free indexes to the remaining released censuses (1841 to 1911) for England and Wales – although you may need to consult a subscription website to see the full transcription online.

There are lots of places to search for census data from England and Wales for a fee. Ancestry and Findmypast have the census material from 1841 to 1911 inclusive, Findmypast is the official TNA partner for the 1901 and 1911 censuses, and TheGenealogist also offers various census transcripts and images from 1841 to 1911.

Most local and county record offices and libraries hold microfilm copies of the census returns for their own area (excluding 1911), and of course many family history societies have produced transcriptions of local census material and other census-like sources. (Glamorgan FHS, for example, has transcribed the aforementioned 1837 and 1839 Town Surveys of Swansea.) In addition, most archives and libraries offer free access to websites such as Ancestry, meaning you can also search nationwide census material. The network of Family History Centres operated by the Church of Jesus Christ of Latter-Day Saints (LDS Church) also offers census material on microfilm.

Finally, although the data is far from complete, you can search partial census transcripts for England, Wales and Scotland free of charge on FreeCEN (freecen.org.uk). Its creators are currently focusing efforts on creating a searchable database of the nineteenth-century census returns.

The Census in Scotland
Census returns for Scotland are almost identical in format to those for England and Wales, except for 1911, when similarly detailed information was gathered, but was then copied into

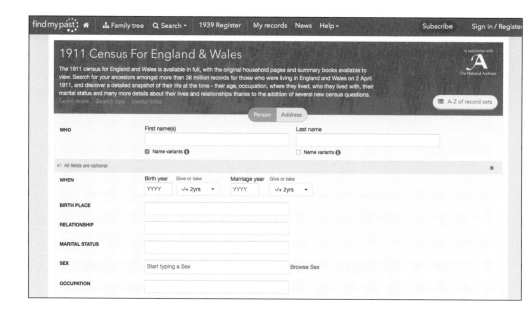

Findmypast's 1911 census page. The website also has unique census substitute the 1939 Register – a snapshot of the country on the eve of war.

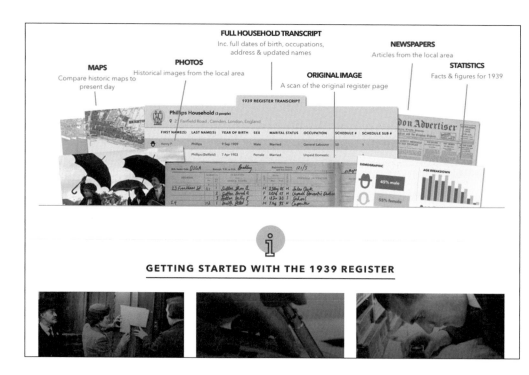

enumeration books as in previous years. This was the twelfth census of Scotland and it was taken on the night of Sunday, 2 April. In the same manner as previous censuses, enumerators were appointed to distribute household schedules within their allocated enumeration district. The completed household schedules were then used as a reference to complete the enumeration books. Around 9,000 enumerators with the ability to 'write well' were appointed to carry out the census.

An enumeration district comprised an area of between 200 and 300 houses, assuming that the enumerator did not have to travel more than about 15 miles visiting each house. An institution comprising normally more than 100 people constituted its own enumeration district. All people who were alive after midnight on the 2 April 1911 were enumerated and people on board boats or barges were enumerated if the vessel was 'within the limits of the jurisdiction of His Majesty's Customs'.

In terms of access to the census returns for Scotland between 1841 and 1911, the situation is much more simple: you use the ScotlandsPeople website, which has indexes and images of the census records. In 2016 the contract for the running of the ScotlandsPeople website was being handed over to a new provider, which may see changes to prices or the way the website works. But at the time of writing it costs £7 to search census indexes databases – giving you 30 'page credits' and allows access for a period of one year. Each time you conduct a search you are told how many records have been found, and you have the opportunity to re-define/narrow the search. Then if you decide to display the results, a single page of twenty-five results costs one credit. Then viewing a record image costs five credits.

Again, there are indexes to the Scottish census available through other websites (such as Ancestry and Findmypast, and some others listed later in this chapter), and also, if you're researching in person, you can view microform copies in many archives and local studies libraries.

Surviving Irish Material

While lots of introductions to Irish research focus on what is missing – most nineteenth-century census material – there are some upsides to the situation. The first is that you can explore indexes and view images of the surviving twentieth-century censuses for free online. The second is that the very absence of nineteenth-century census records has fuelled the mass-digitisation of census substitute sources, many of which are also freely accessible online.

A first official census of Ireland was attempted in 1813, but it did not go well. The Commissioners for the 1901 census, in their General Report, laid out this short, sad history: 'This arrangement worked badly, the Grand Juries, from their constitution, not being capable of efficiently superintending the work, and having at their disposal no adequate machinery for its accomplishment . . . [A]fter two years spent in a fruitless endeavour . . . the attempt was abandoned'.

The first successful census of Ireland was taken in 1821 with further censuses at ten-yearly intervals from 1831 through to 1911. No census was taken in 1921 because of the War of Independence and the first census of the population of the Irish Free State was taken in 1926, and has since been taken in 1926, 1936, 1946, 1951, 1956, 1961, 1966, 1971, 1979, 1981, 1986, 1991, 1996, 2002 and 2006. The next set of Irish census returns to appear, that of the 1926 census, will be released in January 2027.

The original census returns for 1861 and 1871 were destroyed shortly after the censuses were taken, while those for 1881 and 1891 were pulped. Then the returns for 1821, 1831, 1841 and 1851 were (apart from a few survivals) destroyed in 1922 in the fire at the Public Record Office at the beginning of the Civil War.

That's the depressing news over and done with. The good news is that you can, right now, view and explore digitised and indexed images of the 1901 and 1911 census records for Ireland (including Northern Ireland) on the National Archives of Ireland website at census.nationalarchives.ie. These two surviving censuses, taken on 31 March 1901 and 2 April 1911, recorded first name, surname, relationship to the head of the household, religious denomination, literacy level, age, gender, occupation, marital status, place of birth, the ability to speak or write Irish and specified disabilities.

Via the same website you can also search some pre-1901 census fragments, which include Antrim in 1851, an index to heads of household in Dublin in 1851 and parts of Londonderry (Derry) in 1831. You can also use censusfinder.com/ireland.htm to find various census substitutes such as directories, the aforementioned Griffith's Valuation, tithe applotments and muster rolls. The PRONI website (proni.gov.uk) also has all kinds of useful online records, including street directories and valuation revision books.

REMEMBER

- A census has been taken every ten years since 1801 with the exception of 1941. The 1841 census was the first to list the names of every individual.
- If you think a household is missing from the 1861 census (which has the most gaps), you can confirm missing parishes or districts using the advanced search option in TNA's Discovery catalogue. Enter the keyword 'missing' within RG 9. You can also identify pages that are known to be missing within some enumeration districts by using the exact phrase 'missing pages' within RG 9.
- The 1939 Register is the nearest we have to a census of England and Wales between 1921 and 1951. The 1931 census for England and Wales was destroyed during the Second World War and no census was taken in 1941.
- The 1911 census was also the first where the army overseas was enumerated – previously there was only a headcount.

- The census dates: 1841 (6 June), 1851 (30 March), 1861 (7 April), 1871 (2 April), 1881 (3 April), 1891 (5 April), 1901 (31 March), 1911 (2 April), 1921 (19 June).
- House numbers were rarely given in earlier census years, and in rural areas you will often find only the name of the village or hamlet.
- The census asked about language spoken in Wales, from 1891, and in the Isle of Man, from 1901.
- The 1921 census, and all later censuses that survive, are kept by the Office for National Statistics. These censuses will only be available 100 years after the date they were conducted.
- A census of Ireland was first attempted in 1813, but 'after two years spent in a fruitless endeavour . . . was abandoned'.
- Your motto should always be: don't rely on the transcription – check the actual image/document.
- If you can't find someone in one online census index, try another. And if you are failing to find an individual make sure you have tried all the spelling variations (taking into account transcriptions errors).

ONLINE RESOURCES

The National Archives:
  blog.nationalarchives.gov.uk/blog/missing-from-the-census/
Audrey Collins's excellent summary of reasons why someone might be missing from the census, with tips about what to do. There's also the census research guide at nationalarchives. gov.uk/records/research-guides/census-returns.htm.
ScotlandsPeople: scotlandspeople.gov.uk
Hosts census returns for Scotland from 1841 to 1911. It costs £7 to search the census indexes, which includes thirty page credits for viewing images of the original enumerator's pages (images cost five credits each).
Census of Ireland 1901/1911: census.nationalarchives.ie

Here you can search the census of Ireland from 1901 and 1911, and explore surviving fragments (and substitutes) for previous years, all free of charge. All thirty-two counties (for 1901 and 1911) are searchable by all information categories.

FreeCEN: freecen.org.uk

Provides partial census data from the years 1841, 1851, 1861, 1871 and 1891. The focus at present is 1891.

The Domesday Book: opendomesday.org/name/

Explore names recorded in the survey.

UK BMD: ukbmd.org.uk

Use the side menu to navigate to the page listing sites that provide online transcriptions of census material.

1939 Register: findmypast.co.uk

Register of 40+ million Britons alive on Friday, 29 September 1939. It was compiled shortly after the outbreak of war and used to issue identity cards and organise rationing. It is the only census-like record of the population between 1921 and 1951. Findmypast also has the 1841 to 1911 censuses.

1911 Census: 1911census.co.uk

This includes a free searchable index. You can subscribe via Findmypast or buy credits.

1901 Census: 1901censusonline.com Contains a free searchable index.

Ancestry: search.ancestry.co.uk/search/group/ukicen

TheGenealogist: thegenealogist.co.uk

Protestation Returns, Parliamentary Archives: www.parliament.uk/business/publications/parliamentary-archives/archives-highlights/familyhistory/sources/protestations/

FURTHER READING

Christian, Peter and David Annal. *Census: The Family Historian's Guide*, A&C Black, 2014

Jolly, Emma. *Tracing Your Ancestors Using the Census*, Pen & Sword, 2013

Chapter 3

BUILDING BLOCKS: REGIONAL RECORDS

THE PARISH: BAPTISMS, MARRIAGES AND BURIALS

Alongside civil registration and the census, parish material, and more specifically parish registers, forms the third big genealogical source. Together they can prove links between generations (via baptisms) and between branches of the family (via marriages), and in England, Wales and Scotland in particular take your research back well beyond the start of civil registration. Indeed, they can potentially help you trace your line back to the sixteenth century – although this is rare in practice.

Tracking down civil registration records and census material is, in theory at least, relatively straightforward. For parish level sources in particular, the situation is more complicated. But it is worth the effort – there's nothing quite liking seeing original registers, reading the handwriting and sometimes comments from the clergy who presided over the baptism, marriage or burial of an ancestor, sometimes with the marks and signatures of your ancestors and close family. Also, thanks to widespread transcription and indexing, not least by the LDS Church, and the mass county level digitisations through websites such as Ancestry and Findmypast, it's becoming easier to track down parish sources remotely. The situation in Scotland is more advanced in that the equivalent registers, known as Old Parish Register, are available via ScotlandsPeople.

Parish-level records are an exciting area for genealogists. In this first section of this chapter we will be looking at material relating to birth, marriage and death. In the next section we will look in more detail at other parish-level sources, sometimes referred to as 'parish chest' material, as well as the related BMD sources such as marriage banns and licences and burial records.

As explored in Chapter 1, 'The State and the Parish', the way that parish, borough, city, hundred and county administration hangs together can cause confusion. The East Riding of Yorkshire's archives service, based at the Treasure House in Beverley, looks after parish registers for the East Riding Archdeaconry – but as ecclesiastical boundaries are different to local authority boundaries, the Archdeaconry does *not* cover the whole of the East Riding. And this situation is not unique – most regions can offer up their own idiosyncrasies.

In built-up, urban areas identifying the correct parish and where that parish material is likely to reside is even more critical. The London Metropolitan Archives, for example, holds some 17,000 parish registers from more than 700 Church of England parishes, covering central and north-west London. But, as the 'Metropolitan' archives it covers only certain parts of the city – they have no City of Westminster parish registers at all, and many Greater London parish material resides in smaller borough collections. Thankfully, LMA's parish material is arranged alphabetically by borough, and much of it is available through an ongoing digitisation partnership with ancestry.co.uk.

Some of the best advice is often the most obvious. It is generally a good idea to look both ways before stepping out into the road, for example. And although this may seem equally obvious, my one piece of advice is to make sure you are certain of the parish in which your ancestor lived – especially if you are visiting an archive in person. Most local and county archives, and many regional family history societies, provide online guides to their parish holdings and coverage. It really is worth the time investment to explore these thoroughly as you get to know an area.

Keeping Parish Registers

Parish records were originally generated by and preserved at the parish church. In 1538, parish priests were told to start keeping record of all baptisms, marriages and burials during the week. The new records were to be kept in a 'sure coffer' with two locks. And it is these boxes, many of which still survive in parish churches, that has lead to the term 'parish chest material' being used to describe all kinds of parish sources.

The system took time to bed in. To begin with not everyone took it seriously, fearing the paperwork would lead to further taxes being levied on the Church. Plus many kept the records in a haphazard way, on loose sheets of paper, until further decrees ordered that they kept the records in bound books. So, while there are survivals right back to the late 1530s, 1558 is usually seen as the birth date of the parish register as this was the year of a royal proclamation that records should be kept on parchment, meaning more have survived.

To begin with, single registers contained all events. Essex Record Office looks after some really fine early parish registers. One example from Chelmsford, dating from May 1543, mixes baptisms, marriages and burials together in one sequence, with the writer putting a key in the margin: 'C' for christening, 'M' for marriage and 'O' probably for 'obit' (Latin for '(s)he died'). The page also has occasional use of red ink which is unexplained, although local archivists suspect that it may reflect the social status of the parties. William Mildmay, for example, whose baptism appears in red, was a member of Chelmsford's most prominent family.

External influences, particularly the Civil War, resulted in gaps and the detail entered varies depending on the incumbent or clerk who kept the registers. Hampshire chaplain William Rawlins noted a great deal of information about his parishioners. In the second entry of the page of baptisms and burials for Winchester St Cross with St Faith parish covering the years 1789 to 1791, he notes that a 52-year-old woman was for 'several years Cook' at the almshouse St Cross Hospital, while Robert Page, 'a truly pious and good man', had been porter there. Overleaf we have the most extraordinary of entries where he describes the burial of Richard Hart, a Brother of St Cross, in a coffin made by himself out of a Spanish man-of-war he bought while working as a carpenter at Portsmouth Dock twenty years before. Further we learn that he kept the coffin in his room, drawn up on pulleys to the ceiling and 'had painted funeral processions, skulls and other emblems of mortality' on the side. He goes on: 'Brother Hart was a man of a very singular turn and disposition.' He ends the same page from 1791 with an entry for 60-year-old pauper widow Martha Dubber. He adds: 'Her husband, in 1780, was crushed to death by the fall of earth in a sand pit.'

Another example from Essex is the register for the parish of Stansted Mountfitchet covering the years 1609 to 1610, which again has all the hallmarks of the period – tricky handwriting, marriage entries that simply name two parties involved, baptism entries that name the father but not the mother. However, it also boasts an extraordinarily long-delayed entry. At the top of the right-hand page of baptisms from 1610, a later hand has inserted: 'John Burnet the old baylif of Stansted Hall was born this year who lived 90 years, or very near, dying Oct. the 27th 1699.'

You'll sometimes come across pointed digs at parishioners – imagine the character of Mr Collins from Jane Austen's *Pride and Prejudice*, and you'll get the idea. Also, some vicars took it upon themselves to note down all kinds of details they were not strictly required to record. Travel to Meirionnydd Record Office in Gwynedd, Wales, and you'll find a burial register that has notes in the side margin describing the sinking of the ship *Wapela* on the night of 24 January 1868. Many of those lost are noted in the register, including Captain Isaac Lincoln Orr, whose body was later disinterred and sent to North America. And the final entry on the page from the year 1844 records the burial of a young black cabin boy whose body was found washed up on the shore. As the boy's name was unknown, the burial entry reads simply 'Bottle of Beer' – as one was found in his jacket pocket.

Similarly, the Borthwick Institute in York, which looks after the huge York Diocesan Archive, has a Pocklington burial entry from April 1733 that records: 'Thomas Pelling from Burton Stather in Lincolnshire, a Flying Man who was killed by jumping against the Battlement of the Choir when coming down the Rope from the Steeple.' 'Flying men' were part of a 1730s craze for rope dancing, walking and sliding. (You can find out more via the Institute's blog at borthwickinstitute.blogspot.co.uk/2013/05/is-it-bird-is-it-plane-no-its-flying.html.)

New laws formalised and standardised the system over time. One important development for genealogists occurred in 1597, when an Act of Parliament ordered the keeping of what are known as Bishop's Transcripts. These were contemporary copies of the parish registers, made by local clergy and then sent to the bishop of the diocese. Today they offer the frustrated genealogist a second chance – where you find a gap in the parish records, it may often be the case that the Bishop's Transcripts come to the rescue. Although remember that the Bishop's Transcripts sometimes had less detail than the original registers.

It was tradition but not law that marriages should take place in the home parish, but clandestine marriages were commonplace. This was curtailed by Hardwicke's Marriage Act, passed in 1754. The wonderfully named Nottinghamshire clergyman the Revd W. Sweetapple was notorious for marrying couples from near and far at his Fledborough parish church. Check the Fledborough parish register and the number of marriages appearing in the register drops dramatically after the passing of Hardwicke's Marriage Act.

The marriage register from Ashen, a rural parish on the Suffolk border, stops short in 1753. This is because Hardwicke's Marriage Act laid down a single, compulsory form of entry, so that most

Wedding dresses can give clues about when a marriage took place. Once you have found the correct marriage register entry it should include signatures of brides, grooms and witnesses.

parishes acquired a new marriage register in 1754. After the Act marriage registers included signatures of brides, grooms and witnesses, and the clear distinction made between marriages by banns and by licence.

Baptism registers had their formats fixed by an Act of 1812, usually called Rose's Act. For the first time, fathers' occupations were recorded systematically. There was no requirement to record the child's date of birth, but clergymen sometimes squeezed the information in.

The same Act also formalised burial registers. Burial entries can be disappointingly brief: they rarely name any of the deceased's relatives, or give any clue as to where in the churchyard the grave actually lies. 'Abode', during this period, is usually simply the name of the parish. Finally, the year 1837 brought the introduction of a pattern of marriage register still essentially in use today. The most useful addition for family historians is probably the fathers' names and occupations.

There were still regional variations. The Borthwick Institute, which holds parish records for the modern archdeaconry of York – York City parishes and those parishes within approximately a 20-mile radius of the city – is home to the so-called 'Dade registers'. These were a more rigorous and detailed form of record keeping introduced by York clergyman William Dade to three York parishes in the early 1770s, before being adopted more generally across the diocese. Full Dade baptism registers provide the child's name and seniority (e.g. fourth child), the father's name, abode, profession and descent (including the paternal grandparents' names and abode, the grandfather's occupation, and details of the paternal great-grandfather), and the mother's name and descent (including the maternal grandfather's name, abode and occupation and the maternal grandmother's name and descent). Dade burial registers are also of particular interest as they include the age and cause of death.

Another example is the 'Barrington registers', named after the Lord Bishop of Salisbury, the Rt Revd Shute Barrington. In the diocese of Durham between 1798 and 1812, he ordered that more detailed information should be kept in baptism and burial registers. Between these dates each baptism entry should give the date of baptism, name of the child, date of birth, position in the family, the occupation and abode of the father, and the maiden name and place of origin of the mother. Burial registers give the name and abode of the deceased, his parentage, occupation, the date of death, date of burial and age.

Scotland and Ireland

In Scotland parish registers are referred to as Old Parish Registers, or OPRs. These were maintained by parishes of the Established Church – the Church of Scotland – usually by the parish minister or session clerk. The National Records of Scotland holds the surviving original registers and these are accessible via the ScotlandsPeople website.

As with the early system south of the border, to begin with there was no standardised format, so you will find a great deal of variation. The relevant ScotlandsPeople page warns that information may be 'sparse, unreliable and difficult to read'. The oldest surviving register dates from 1553 (the baptisms and banns from Errol in Perthshire), but while there was a requirement from 1552 that parishes record baptisms and marriages, many did not commence until much later, partly because registration was costly and unpopular. Also, while some Nonconformists can be found in these registers, many chose to have events registered in their own churches.

In Ireland, with so little surviving census material from the nineteenth century, the parish registers take on even more importance. Indeed, for many researchers they offer the only potential source for tracing an individual.

In the 1950s and 1960s, the National Library of Ireland microfilmed registers from the majority of Catholic parishes in

The National Library of Ireland website (registers.nli.ie) where you can search digitised Catholic parish registers from the majority of Catholic parishes in Ireland and Northern Ireland up to 1880.

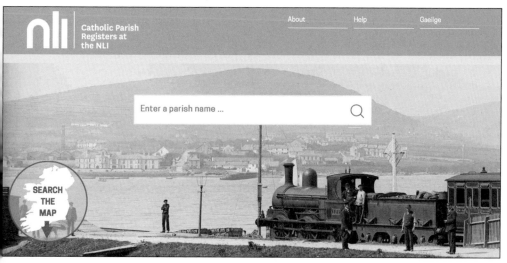

Ireland and Northern Ireland. The registers contain records of baptisms and marriages from the majority of Catholic parishes up to 1880. Digital images from these microfilms are now freely available on the website Catholic Parish Registers at the NLI: registers.nli.ie. The start dates of the registers vary from the 1740/1750s in some city parishes in Dublin, Cork, Galway, Waterford and Limerick to the 1780/1790s in counties such as Kildare, Wexford, Waterford and Kilkenny. Registers for parishes along the western seaboard do not generally begin until the 1850/1860s.

Catholic christenings generally took place as soon as possible after children were born, sometimes on the same day. The records include the date of baptism, names of child, father and mother (with maiden surname in later records), and the sponsors or godparents. Some christening records also include the child's birth date and the family's place of residence.

Marriage records normally provide the date of the marriage, the names of the bride and groom, and the names of the witnesses. Occasionally, places of residence are listed. Meanwhile, burials would record the name of the deceased, date of burial and sometimes an occupation or residence (townland). Later years often include the age at death and for children at least one of the names of the parents, usually the father.

There are also Church of Ireland (Anglican Church) parochial records, which often remain with the relevant parishes. It is estimated that they survive for about one-third of the parishes throughout the country. Many registers (originals, copies and microfilmed examples) are held in the National Archives of Ireland. PRONI also holds copies of surviving Church of Ireland registers for the dioceses of Armagh, Clogher, Connor, Derry, Dromore, Down, Kilmore and Raphoe.

Accessing Parish Registers

Registers were originally kept by the church, but most have since now been deposited in diocesan archives or county record offices, often accessible as microform copies in archives and local libraries.

Genealogists and academic societies have been transcribing and indexing parish registers since Victorian times, and many groups and societies produced printed transcripts and indexes – such as the Parish Register Society, the Harleian Society, Phillimore & Co. and the Society of Genealogists.

Regional genealogical groups have also produced transcriptions, indexes and other finding aids. Indeed, one important national project, overseen by the Federation of Family History Societies, was the National Burial Index (NBI). This groundbreaking project led to the first published edition of the NBI in 2001, containing some 5.4 million records, derived mainly from registers and Bishop's Transcripts. The NBI has since gone through several editions and is now available online via Findmypast (the majority of the records cover the period from 1813 to 1850).

Lots of microform copies of parish material are available through Family History Centres run by the LDS Church, which also preserves the mind-boggling collections at the Family History Library in Salt Lake City. The LDS Church also produced the International Genealogical Index (the IGI), which includes indexed data mainly from baptisms and marriages. This is available online but, as with all transcriptions, should always be used with caution, as errors can occur in legibility of the original document or the microfilm copy.

In more recent years FamilySearch has continued partnerships with regional archives and commercial partners to further digitise parish-level material. Durham University Palace Green Library, for example, looks after Bishop's Transcripts of County Durham and Northumberland parish registers from between 1760 and 1840. Images of these transcripts are all available through FamilySearch. (You can find out more about this and other family history sources via the Library's dedicated genealogical portal familyrecords.dur.ac.uk.)

There's lot of material online, but also lots of regional variation. In Yorkshire, for example, the situation is changing rapidly as millions of baptism, marriage and burial register entries are coming to findmypast.co.uk through agreements with six Yorkshire archives. At the time of writing, around 2,700 parish registers from over 250 parishes in the dioceses of York, Bradford and Ripon and Leeds were being digitised. Meanwhile, the site already boasts the Staffordshire Collection, which, when complete, will comprise around 6 million searchable transcripts/images covering all Anglican parish registers up to 1900, and including Stoke-on-Trent and parishes now within the City of Wolverhampton, as well as the Boroughs of Dudley, Sandwell and Walsall. Meanwhile, volunteers are busy creating and adding to indexes on the dedicated Staffordshire Name Indexes site (www.staffsnameindexes.org.uk). You should also look out for 'online parish clerks' projects, which often transcribe and provide parish-level data free of charge. Cornwall Online Parish Clerks, for example, can be found at cornwall-opc.org.

Some more useful websites with parish register transcriptions and finding aids are listed below.

REMEMBER
- Parish registers often survive back to the mid-sixteenth century. The earliest register entries were often little more than lists of names. Parish registers were gradually standardised through Acts of 1753 and 1812.
- Nonconformist and other non-parochial births and baptisms, deaths and burials (and some marriages) can be searched via www.BMDregisters.co.uk.
- Most Nonconformists were required by law to marry in Church of England churches between 1754 and 1837. So you may well find records of them in Anglican parish registers.

- TNA holds Clandestine Marriages & Baptisms in the Fleet Prison, King's Bench Prison, the Mint & the May Fair Chapel ranging from 1667 to *c.* 1777.
- There are alternative sources of BMD data – *The Gentleman's Magazine*, for example, founded in 1731 and running for almost 200 years, would often include lists of births, marriages, deaths, bankruptcies and military promotions.

ONLINE RESOURCES

ScotlandsPeople: scotlandspeople.gov.uk
Offers access to Old Parish Registers and Catholic Registers from across Scotland.

FamilySearch: familysearch.org
Hosts the International Genealogical Index (IGI), a mass parish-level source first published as a computer file in 1973. There are also vast indexes, transcriptions and register images for other parts of the UK.

FreeREG: freereg.org.uk
Volunteer led drive to provide free online searches of transcribed parish and Nonconformist registers.

National Library of Wales: llgc.org.uk
Has parish registers from over 500 parishes on microfilm in the South Reading Room. It also has archives of the Church in Wales (excluding original parish registers but including Bishop's Transcripts). Findmypast has a significant Wales Collection of parish material.

National Library of Ireland: nli.ie
The NLI has made its collection of Catholic parish register microfilms freely available via registers.nli.ie.

National Records of Scotland: nationalrecordsofscotland.gov.uk

PRONI: proni.gov.uk

Ancestry: ancestry.co.uk/parish

Essex Ancestors: seax.essexcc.gov.uk/EssexAncestors.aspx

The Essex Record Office digital gateway to various sources including parish registers.

Findmypast: findmypast.co.uk

The Genealogist: thegenealogist.co.uk/parish_records/

Datasets include the noted Phillimore transcripts of marriages, as well as it has various regional collections – it recently announced a new agreement to digitise Norfolk parish/historical records.

Parish Chest: parishchest.com

Lincs to the Past: www.lincstothepast.com/help/parish-registers/

Access Lincolnshire parish registers.

Federation of Family History Societies: ffhs.org.uk

London Registers: www.parishregister.com

Specialises in parish data covering London, particularly from the Docklands.

UK BMD: ukbmd.org.uk

Useful lists of online parish data including Online Parish Clerk websites such as Dorset Online Parish Clerks (opcdorset.org), Cornwall (www.cornwall-opc-database.org) and Kent (kent-opc.org).

Sheffield Indexers: sheffieldindexers.com/ParishBaptismIndex.html

Cumberland & Westmorland Parish Registers: cumberlandarchives.co.uk

THE PARISH CHEST

'Parish chest records' refer to parish-level records that were traditionally stored in a parish chest or strong box. These include the likes of vestry minutes, churchwardens' accounts and Poor Law material. Some parish chest records, such as bastardy bonds and records of Overseers of the Poor are explored in more detail in Chapter 4, 'Secrets, Scandals and Hard Times', while

Fontmell Magna church, where my parents were married, my grandfather was churchwarden and I was mistaken for a girl.

apprenticeship records appear in Chapter 4, 'Working Lives'. Here we're going to explore not only these parish-level records, but also some of the alternative sources relating to marriages and deaths.

Vestry Minutes and Churchwarden's Accounts

Many genealogists ignore other parish chest material as they are not nearly so likely to have been indexed or transcribed, so accessing and exploring them is time consuming. But they can provide you with a vivid picture of the workings of the local community, about the life of a parish.

The earliest surviving parish records are often the accounts of churchwardens. Their chief responsibility was the maintenance of the church building and its contents. That may sound unpromising from a genealogical perspective, but sometimes they offer more than you might expect. A page of accounts for Great Dunmow in 1538, held at Essex Record Office, includes a list of rents and other receipts, headed by 41 shillings gathered at Christmas by the Lord of Misrule, William Stuard. There's also a list of subscribers towards 'the greate bell clapper' – most men contributed a penny or less, although three widows were also named on the list.

Churchwardens were also responsible to the bishop or magistrate for presenting any wrongdoings at quarter sessions, including failure to attend church, drunkenness or other undesirable behaviour. You can explore the kinds of cases that might reach the Diocesan Courts via the wonderful Cause Papers Database at www.hrionline.ac.uk/causepapers/. These are from the Archbishopric of York and span the years 1300 to 1858; the originals are held in the Borthwick Institute for Archives at the University of York. A simple search by the word 'churchwarden' resulted in a case from October 1556, when Robert Fox, the vicar's clerk at St Martin le Grande, Coney Street, York, was accused of drunkenness, neglect of duty, quarrelling and brawling. The plaintiffs were churchwardens Nicholas Havelock, Richard Aneley and William Newsam.

Vestry minutes are essentially the minutes of the parish council, and will include lots of names of individuals and references to appointments, as well as agreements of care and lists of parishioners such as men eligible for parish duties and details of illegitimate children. These will often include Overseers of the Poor records.

Overseers Records

Overseers accounts, like the vestry minutes, record payments made to the poor and rates charged and received. In January 1800 the monthly meeting of the Hornchurch vestry (today part of the London borough of Havering) faced heavy bills for poor relief.

And overseers accounts like these provide vivid evidence of life at the bottom of the heap between the seventeenth and early nineteenth centuries. Quite apart from the names of individual paupers, they are also a good source for local tradespeople – recording payments to people employed by the parish in various capacities, such as molecatchers, blacksmiths and slaters.

Settlement, Bastardy and Pauper Apprentices
Until the passing of the New Poor Law, the parish was responsible for the welfare of its parishioners. Therefore, before spending money on an individual in dire need, parish administrators wanted to be sure the person was from that parish – and they would often go to some lengths to prove someone was not their responsibility.

These records derive from the Act of Settlement and Removal (1662) which established the need to prove entitlement to poor relief by issuing Settlement Certificates. The certificates proved which parish a family belonged to and therefore which parish had the legal responsibility to provide poor relief if needed. In some cases, if a person was about to or had become a burden on the parish, a Settlement Examination would be carried out to determine whether the person had a legitimate right to residency and relief. If it was found they did not, they would be served a Removal Order. Settlement examinations in particular can be very enlightening as they give mini-biographies of those applying for poor relief. In addition, they can often give you clues about which parish to search next for records of the individual. (There's a really useful guide to Settlement Certificates and removal orders at: genguide.co.uk/source/settlement-certificatesexaminations-and-removal-orders-parish-amp-poor-law/173/.)

Similarly, records of bastardy were created during a process in which the parish would try to establish the father of an illegitimate child, so the father, and not the parish, could provide for that child. You can find out more about the so-called bastardy bonds in Chapter 4, 'Secrets, Scandals and Hard Times'. In the meantime, to explore some examples try London Lives (londonlives.org) which has a number of case studies and databases drawn from London collections, including bastardy examinations and pauper settlements.

Apprenticeship records are dealt with in Chapter 4, 'Working Lives', but in short, so-called pauper apprenticeships were arranged specifically to remove the child as a financial burden on the parish. (Unlike

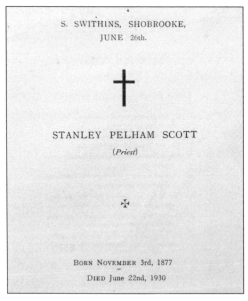

S. SWITHINS, SHOBROOKE,

JUNE 26th.

✝

STANLEY PELHAM SCOTT

(*Priest*)

✠

BORN NOVEMBER 3rd, 1877

DIED June 22nd, 1930

DEATH OF SIR WILLIAM FRY

LIFE-LONG FRIEND OF DR. BARNARDO

We regret to report the death, which took place at his home, Nevin, Hook Heath, Woking, on Friday last week, of Sir William Fry. He was aged 86.

Sir William, who was formerly solicitor to the Woods, Forests and Land Revenues, Ireland, became well-known in this country as chairman of Dr. Barnardo's Homes and an active supporter of the work of many philanthropic institutions. He was knighted in 1915 for his philanthropic services and came to live in retirement at Hook Heath.

Born in Dublin in 1853, Sir William came from an old-established family of solicitors there, the practice of Messrs. William Fry and Sons having been established for more than 100 years. He was admitted a solicitor in Dublin in 1874, having taken first-class honours in the final examination. He was afterwards the president of the Incorporated Law Society of Ireland from 1895-96.

Sir William was a member of the British Association, Fellow of the Royal Geographical Society, and a member of the Royal Irish Academy. He also attained the honour of being Deputy Lieutenant for Dublin and was a Fellow of the Royal Statistical Society of Ireland. Other offices which he held were those of chairman of the Solicitors' Benevolent Association of Ireland, chairman of the Royal Hospital for Incurables of Ireland, governor of the Royal Hibernian Memorial School, member of the committee of the Society for the Prevention of Cruelty to Children and vice-patron of the Masonic Children's School. During the war Sir William served as the hon. treasurer for the Dublin Prince of Wales's National Relief Fund, and was at one time a Government visitor to the Mountjoy Convict Prison.

An important position which he held for many years was that of deputy chairman of the Dr. Barnardo's Homes. Dr. Barnardo also came from Dublin and was the teacher of the Sunday School class to which Sir William belonged. The two were life-long friends. Sir William has always been greatly interested in all forms of practical philanthropy and a position he held was that of chair of the Mission to Lepers. He was keenly interested in and did much good work for the Y.M.C.A.

Sir William Fry celebrated his golden wedding in 1926. His wife died two years ago. There were five children of the marriage, two sons and three daughters.

Two valuable pieces of evidence from the author's family archive. The order of service for the funeral of the Revd Stanley Pelham Scott, which took place in Shobrooke, Devon in June 1930, and a newspaper cutting with the obituary of a forebear – Dublin-born philanthropist Sir William Fry.

trade apprenticeships, the pauper apprentice indentures were not subject to stamp duty.) This was a feature of the Old Poor Law which allowed the parish officials to bind children as young as 7 to a master. The agreements were drawn up between an apprentice and a master, overseen by the parish, and indentures may survive, or apprentice agreements can be found in the vestry or Overseer of the Poor minutes.

Some county collections of these types of records have already been digitised and are available through commercial websites. Some archives have also catalogued and indexed their collections. The website and catalogue of Gloucestershire Archives, for example, has a useful online Genealogical Database, which includes names in the pre-1834 parish overseers' records – including settlement, apprenticeship and bastardy records. (See www.gloucestershire.gov.uk/archives/article/107400/Genealogical -database.)

Monumental Inscriptions and Cemetery Records

Away from the parish chest, there are other potential sources relating to death and burial. Surviving gravestones, for example, can contain information not found elsewhere. They may mention family relationships, will usually confirm dates of birth and death. They can also allow you to make deductions about a family's relative wealth and status, and may even include designs or heraldic devices that may offer further clues.

Genealogical groups across Britain and Ireland have been transcribing and recording these sources for years, and while some of the data is only available in booklet form, many more can be accessed via CDs, often with images of the original stones. Others have free online indexes to a centralised monumental inscriptions database, and still others have entered partnerships with commercial bodies – including specialists such as DeceasedOnline.

Before the 1850s the vast majority of burials were recorded in the registers of Anglican parish churches (although some Nonconformist chapels had their own burial grounds). An Act of Parliament in 1853 enabled local authorities or private companies to purchase and use land for the purpose of burial.

DeceasedOnline is a good place to view other types of burial records from major municipal cemeteries across England, Wales and Scotland. Again, it's also worth checking the local authority website as some provide free access to burial records. You may find the likes of this service offered at the Kingston upon Thames Burial Records site, kingston.gov.uk/info/200136/funerals_cremations_and_cemeteries/342/search_our_burial_records), where you can search records from July 1855 to December 2003. While at Belfast Burials (belfastcity.gov.uk/community/burialrecords/burialrecords.aspx) you can search

Some local authorities have put municipal burial and cremation records online. This example from Manchester can be explored at www.burialrecords.manchester. gov.uk.

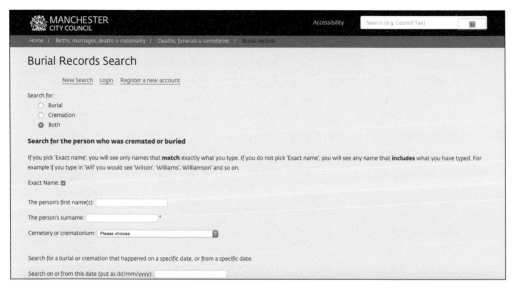

360,000 Belfast burial records from 3 cemeteries dating back to 1869, and buy images of burial records for £1.50 each. Another useful site is Gravestone Photos (gravestonephotos.com), a growing photographic resource launched in 1998, aiming to photograph and index monuments across the globe (coverage is dominated by England and Scotland).

Marriage Banns and Bonds

The banns of marriage, commonly known simply as the 'banns', are the public announcement in a Christian parish church or in the town council of an impending marriage. Their purpose was to give anyone the opportunity to raise any potential impediment to the marriage.

There were many reasons why individuals might want to marry secretly or in a hurry – if the bride was pregnant or if the groom was on military leave perhaps. Differences in social standing, Nonconformism or simple family opposition to a union might all stand in the way of traditional weddings.

The Church allowed them to circumnavigate the unwanted publicity of calling banns on three successive Sundays by providing a marriage licence – for a fee. And the information given in order to obtain the licence may include detail not available elsewhere. From the early seventeenth century a person applying for the licence (usually the groom) had to provide a bond and an allegation. The allegation was a formal statement containing ages, marital status and places of residence, with an oath that there was no formal impediment to marriage. Then the bond was sworn by witnesses, one of whom pledged to forfeit a sum of money should there prove to be any fraud.

Survival of banns, licences and bonds is patchy, but just as Bishop's Transcripts can offer a second chance for genealogists looking for parish material, so these related marriage records can give you more opportunities to trace a legal marriage. Where they reside varies, but much of the material may be held in diocesan collections. Through the online catalogue of the National Library of Wales website, for example, you can search some 90,000 bonds and affidavits relating to marriages held in Wales between 1616 and 1837. Similarly, the University of Nottingham's Manuscripts and Special Collections Department houses a heavily used collection of bonds and allegations for marriage licences granted by the Archdeaconry Court of Nottingham from 1594 to 1884. And the aforementioned Borthwick Institute for Archives, home to one of the oldest diocesan collections in the country, houses both Bishop's Transcripts stretching back to 1598 and marriage bonds.

FamilySearch, Ancestry, Findmypast, TheGenealogist and more all boast marriage banns, licences and bonds from various areas. Findmypast's Staffordshire Collection, which was launched with parish registers between 1538 and 1900, later expanded to include Diocese of Lichfield marriage bonds and allegations. And as the diocese was wider than just Staffordshire, this benefits family historians researching families from Derbyshire, north Shropshire and north Warwickshire.

In Scotland too the proclamation of banns was the notice of contract of marriage, read out in the kirk before the marriage took place. Couples or their 'cautioners' (sponsors) were often required to pay a 'caution' or security to prove the seriousness of their intentions. And forthcoming marriages were supposed to be proclaimed on three successive Sundays, however, in practice, all three proclamations could be made on the same day on payment of a fee. All this and more detail about Scottish OPR Banns and Marriages can be found via the relevant ScotlandsPeople page (you'll find the link on the left-hand homepage menu).

ONLINE RESOURCES

Parish Chest Records:
familysearch.org/learn/wiki/en/Parish_Chest_Records

Ancestry: ancestry.co.uk/parish

ScotlandsPeople: scotlandspeople.gov.uk

Findmypast: search.findmypast.co.uk/search-united-kingdom-
records-in-birth-marriage-death-and-parish-records

Bishop'sTranscripts, Devon Archives:
devon.gov.uk/bishops_transcripts.htm

Deceased Online: deceasedonline.com

Leading commercial specialists, providing data from graveyards
and municipal cemeteries across the UK.

Gloucestershire Archives, Genealogical Database:
www.gloucestershire.gov.uk/archives/article/107400/Genealog
ical-database.

Anguline Research Archives: anguline.co.uk

Republishes rare books on CD/PDF download, including many
volumes of UK parish transcriptions.

Gravestone Photos: gravestonephotos.com

Interment: interment.net

Free library of Cemetery Records Online, drawn from
cemeteries and graveyards across the globe.

Burial Inscriptions: burial-inscriptions.co.uk

Sheffield Indexers: sheffieldindexers.com/BurialIndex.html

Death & Burial, GenesReunited:
genesreunited.co.uk/articles/world-records/full-list-of-united-
kingdom-records/births-marriages-and-deaths/deaths-and-
burials

Manchester Burial Records:
www.burialrecords.manchester.gov.uk

Belfast Burials:
belfastcity.gov.uk/community/burialrecords/burialrecords.aspx

GraveMatters: gravematters.org.uk

FURTHER READING

Annal, David and Audrey Collins. *Birth, Marriage and Death Records: A Guide for Family Historians*, Pen & Sword, 2012

Grenham, John. *Tracing Your Irish Ancestors*, Gill & Macmillan, 2012

Heritage, Celia. *Tracing Your Ancestors Through Death Records: A Guide for Family Historians*, Pen & Sword, 2015

Humphery-Smith, Cecil R. *The Phillimore Atlas and Index of Parish Registers*, Phillimore, 2002

Probert, Rebecca. *Marriage Law for Genealogists*, Takeaway Publishing, 2012

Raymond, Stuart A. *Tracing Your Ancestors' Parish Records*, Pen & Sword, 2015

Tate, William Edward. *The Parish Chest*, Phillimore, 2011

Chapter 4

GOING FURTHER

NONCONFORMITY

From the reign of Henry VIII England swung from Catholicism to Protestantism and back to Catholicism. The Act of Supremacy of 1558 re-established the Church of England's independence from Rome, while the Act of Uniformity (passed the following year) set the English Book of Common Prayer at the heart of church services and made it a requirement that everyone had to go to

John Wesley, the theologian who founded the evangelical movement known as Methodism, preaching outside a church.

church once a week or face a fine. The Church of England had broken away from the authority of the Pope and the Roman Catholic Church.

The term 'Nonconformist' derives from just over a century later when more than 2,000 clergymen refused to take the oath after a new Act of Uniformity set out forms of prayers, sacraments and other Church of England rites. This became known as the Great Ejection and created the concept of Nonconformity – the Protestant Christian who did not 'conform'. Some Nonconformists were viewed as radical separatists, as dissenters, and for many years they were restricted from many spheres of public life. Though Catholics and Jews were Nonconformists, the word is normally used to describe Presbyterians, Congregationalists, Baptists, Quakers and Methodists, among others.

The Presbyterian Church of Scotland has been recognised as the national church of Scotland since 1690. Although the relationship between Church and State in Scotland is not the same as in England, 'Nonconformist' is still used to describe churches that are not part of the Church of Scotland, such as Baptist, Methodist or Catholic. In Scotland, before 1834, Nonconformist ministers could not legally perform marriages as clergymen. After 1834 they could, but only if the banns had first been read in the parish church. Total authority was granted in 1855.

There are pockets and patterns in the distribution of Nonconformist churches. During the mid-seventeenth century the main areas of Quakerism, for example, were Westmorland, Cumberland, north Lancashire, Durham and Yorkshire. Wales, in particular, was dominated by the Methodist Church.

The London Metropolitan Archives has one of the largest collections relating to the history of the Anglo-Jewish community in Britain. These include records of organisations that helped individuals such as the Jewish Temporary Shelter and the Jews

Free School. Staying in the capital, Tower Hamlets Local History Library and Archives has records of a number of Nonconformist churches, including material relating to St George's German Lutheran Church (records of which have been comprehensively indexed by the Anglo-German Family History Society). St George's German Lutheran Church, in Alie Street, Whitechapel, is the oldest surviving German Lutheran church in the UK, founded in 1762 by Dietrich Beckman, a wealthy sugar refiner. This area became home to many sugar refiners of German descent and at its height there were an estimated 16,000 German Lutherans in Whitechapel.

Historically, many Nonconformists used their local parish church for registration purposes (even after the Toleration Act of 1689 granted the freedom to worship), but also kept their own registers, particularly for births, baptisms and burials. Between 1754 and 1837 it was illegal to marry anywhere except in a Church of England parish church, unless you were a member of the Society of Friends (Quakers) or Jewish. And after 1837, while

One of the most useful Nonconformist research websites is BMDregisters.co.uk, which has over 8 million BMD records from Quakers (Society of Friends), Methodists, Wesleyans, Baptists, Independents, Protestant Dissenters, Congregationalists, Presbyterians and Unitarians.

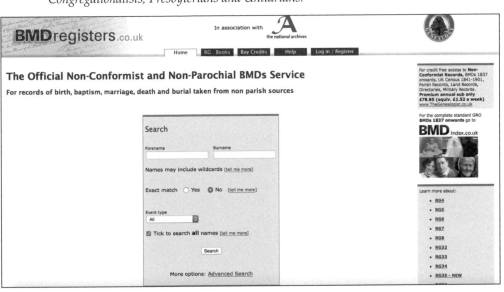

people were now allowed to marry in the church of their choice, some organisations still did not keep their own records.

Although other commercial players have mass Nonconformist collections, the market leader in this area is TheGenealogist.co.uk. It boasts over 8 million birth/baptism, marriage and burial records drawn from TNA, including material from Quakers (Society of Friends), Methodists, Wesleyans, Baptists, Independents, Protestant Dissenters, Congregationalist, Presbyterians and Unitarians. The data is available via subscription or pay-per-view via TheGenealogist or the official BMDregisters.co.uk site. Meanwhile, Ancestry hosts the likes of the London Non-conformist registers (1694–1921) collection, drawn from its partnership with the London Metropolitan Archives.

Baptists

Historians trace the earliest church labelled 'Baptist' back to 1609 in Amsterdam, with English Separatist John Smyth as its pastor. In short, the Baptists believe baptisms should be performed only for professing believers (rather than infants). The first congregation in the UK was established in London in 1612.

You can search the Protestant Dissenters' Registry via BMD registers.co.uk/TheGenealogist. This served the congregations of Baptists, Independents and Presbyterians in London and within a 12-mile radius of the capital. However, parents from most parts of the British Isles and even abroad also used the registry. It was started in 1742, with retrospective entries going back to 1716, and continued until 1837.

Baptist Historical Society: baptisthistory.org.uk
Website has a useful family history page, listing some of the most
    important repositories of Baptist records.
Baptist History & Heritage Society: baptisthistory.org/bhhs/

Catholics

In Ireland the largest Christian denomination is Roman Catholicism, followed by the Anglican Church of Ireland. Catholic parish registers for the majority of Catholic registers in Ireland were microfilmed in the 1950s and 1960s by the National Library of Ireland. Today digital images from these microfilms are now freely available on the website: registers.nli.ie. Many Church of Ireland registers of baptisms, marriages and burials were destroyed, especially in the fire at PRONI in 1922. Some of the survivors have been digitised and are available via the expanding Anglican Record Project at www.ireland.anglican.org/arp.

After the Reformation in Scotland, the greatly reduced Catholic population was concentrated in three main areas Dumfries-shire and Kirkcudbright, Moray and Aberdeenshire, Inverness-shire and the Western Isles, although Edinburgh and Glasgow also attracted many Irish catholic immigrants.

ScotlandsPeople has Catholic records from all Scottish parishes in existence by 1855 (the start of civil registration) as well as records of the Catholic cemeteries in Edinburgh and Glasgow. Baptismal registers, for example, often record dates of birth as well as baptism, and name, parents' names (including the mother's maiden surname), place/parish of residence, father's occupation, witnesses (occasionally with relationship to the child) and name of the priest.

In England, following the sixteenth-century Act of Uniformity, Catholics who continued to practise their faith, could face fines, imprisonment and persecution. As a result, very few records were maintained during the seventeenth century – it only became commonplace from the mid-nineteenth century. Catholic registers often give more detail than their Anglican counterparts, and you must always remember that, as with other Non-conformists, Catholics frequently appear in Anglican sources.

BMDregisters.co.uk has the TNA material from RG 4 which include births, baptisms, deaths, burials and marriages for some

Roman Catholic communities in Dorset, Hampshire, Lancashire, Lincolnshire, Northumberland, Nottinghamshire, Oxfordshire and Yorkshire. The majority cover Northumberland. Most Catholic registers, however, remain in the custody of the parish.

Catholic National Library: catholic-library.org.uk
Hosts a vast library and many transcribed mission registers (listing baptisms, confirmations, marriages and deaths).
Catholic Family History Society: www.catholic-history.org.uk/ cfhs/
The Society has produced a large number of transcriptions. One randomly picked example is the 'Registers of the Sardinian Embassy Chapel, London 1772–1841'. This contains transcriptions with indexes of twelve baptismal registers from the Sardinian Chapel in Lincoln's Inn Fields, known as 'the Mother Church of the Catholic faith in the Archdiocese of Westminster'. In total the indexes contain over 60,000 names.
Irish Ancestors:
irishtimes.com/ancestor/browse/records/church/catholic/
Commercial site with large database of material and useful parish map of Roman Catholic records.
Manchester & Lancashire FHS:
mlfhs.org.uk/data/catholic_search.php
Has an index to Catholic parish registers for Manchester.
Scottish Catholic Archives: scottishcatholicarchives.org.uk
Catholic Church for England & Wales: catholic-ew.org.uk
Useful for tracking down details of diocesan archives – such as Leeds Diocesan Archives (dioceseofleeds.org.uk/archives/).

Huguenots

The Huguenots were French Protestants who fled persecution after an edict that had allowed some religious freedoms in France was revoked. They arrived in waves during the seventeenth and eighteenth centuries, establishing communities in England and later Ireland. In 1718 the French Hospital was founded in London, which would become the seat of the Huguenot Society, which began to record the history of Huguenot migration and history.

Many of the refugees were artisans and craftsmen and they established a major weaving industry in and around Spitalfields. There are many French surnames associated with the Huguenots, but also some anglicised their surnames after arriving in Britain.

Again the Huguenot records on BMDregisters/The Genealogist cover parts of London, Middlesex, Essex, Gloucestershire, Kent, Devon and Norfolk. Until 1754 Huguenots often recorded their marriages in both Huguenot and Church of England registers (although none were recorded in Huguenot registers after that date).

Huguenot Society: huguenotsociety.org.uk
The Society has transcribed and published all of the surviving Huguenot church registers. Indexed publications contain hundreds of names of members of Huguenot congregations and communities. You can search for an ancestor via the microfiche index for the first fifty-nine volumes of the Quarto Series, via individual volume indexes. There's also huguenotsinireland.com. The Huguenot Library is currently housed at TNA in Kew. You can also read about the new Huguenot Heritage Centre in Rochester.
Huguenot Museum: huguenotmuseum.org

Jews

Jewish material is spread across a wide range of archives throughout the UK. The London Metropolitan Archives has an important collection and TNA has lots of references to Jews and Jewish communities, although these are often spread across varied record sorties – such as naturalisation records, for example. Or there's the Scottish Jewish Archives Centre, which has synagogue registers of births, marriages and deaths, as well as copies of some circumcision registers.

The Jewish Genealogical Society of Great Britain is the leading light in the area and the website (www.jgsgb.org.uk) has a vast amount of useful information, plus links to important archives, online databases, research tips, news and more. You can also order copies of Marriage Authorisation Certificates for marriages before 1908.

The Jewish Genealogical Society of Great Britain also leads, with JewishGen, the joint Jewish Communities and Records – United Kingdom project (www.jewishgen.org/JCR-uk/). This aims to record details of all Jewish communities and congregations that have ever existed in the UK, as well as in the Republic of Ireland and Gibraltar. Currently, it boasts 7,000 pages covering over 1,000 Jewish congregations.

It has a huge number of databases, from the Bradford Jewish Cemeteries Database to the Merthyr Tydfil Jewish Community, the Caedraw School Register. There's also the vast 1851 Anglo-Jewry Database, which covers mainly England, Wales and Scotland, but also Ireland, the Channel Islands and Isle of Man. Most of the 29,000+ entries appear in the 1851 census and represent 90+ per cent of the Jewish population in the British Isles.

JewishGen Family-Finder: www.jewishgen.org/jgff/
Gives surnames and ancestral towns of more than 500,000 entries, by adding your family details it will increase the chances of linking with other researchers looking for the same surname. There's also the JewishGen Online Worldwide Burial Registry, boasting entries from 4,200 cemeteries and burial records in 83 countries.
Scottish Jewish Archives Centre: sjac.org.uk
Founded in 1987 and based in Scotland's oldest Synagogue – the Garnethill Synagogue in Glasgow. Has synagogue minute books and registers, membership lists, personal papers and photographs. The Archive maintains a collection of Jewish newspapers, which often contain personal announcements.

British-Jewry: www.british-jewry.org.uk
Hosts several databases from the Portsmouth circumcision
    database to the vast Leeds Database.
Judaica Europeana: www.judaica-europeana.eu
Yad Vashem:
www.yadvashem.org/yv/en/remembrance/names/index.asp
Working to recover the names of the 6 million Jews who perished
    in the Holocaust, and adding them to the Central Database of
    Holocaust victims.
Jewish Historical Society of England: jhse.org
USC Shoah Foundation: http://sfi.usc.edu
Beth Shalom Holocaust Web Centre: www.ajex.org.uk
Jewish Museum London: jewishmuseum.org.uk
Manchester Jewish Museum: manchesterjewishmuseum.com

Methodists

Methodism, or the Methodist movement, which actually covers
more than one denomination, was born out of the life and
teachings of John Wesley (1703–91). Both John and his brother,
the hymn writer Charles Wesley, were ordained Anglican clergy.
Methodism was organised by chapels at the centre of large
'circuits' around which particular ministers would preach,
perform baptisms and even marriages (before 1753). The North
Lancashire District, for example, currently comprises eighteen
circuits of town and country churches.

Methodism also spread to Ireland – the first Methodist society
was formed in Dublin in 1746, and John Wesley first visited
Ireland the following year. By the time of his death in 1791 Irish
Methodist membership numbered over 14,000.

Via BMDregisters you can search Wesleyan Methodist Records
from the Wesleyan Methodist Registry, set up in 1818 and
continued until 1838. It provided registration of births and
baptisms of Wesleyan Methodists throughout England and Wales
and elsewhere.

Methodist Historical Society of Ireland:
methodisthistoryireland.org
Maintains an extensive archive relating to Methodism in Ireland,
   including records of individual churches and journals/
   periodicals. The website has a useful index of Irish Methodist
   churches, chapels and preaching houses, as well as guides to
   records such as Irish Methodist baptismal and marriage records.
My Methodist History: mymethodisthistory.org.uk
Community archive network that encourages users to share
   photos and stories. There are also sites My Primitive Methodist
   Ancestors (myprimitivemethodists.org.uk) and My Wesleyan
   Methodist Ancestors (mywesleyanmethodists.org.uk).
Methodist Central Hall: church.methodist-central-hall.org.uk
Contains the names of over 1 million people who donated a
   guinea to the Wesleyan Methodist Twentieth Century Fund
   between 1899 and 1904.
Methodist Archives and Research Centre:
ibrary.manchester.ac.uk/searchresources/guidetospecialcollectio
ns/methodist/
Manchester University's Methodist Archives and Research Centre
   houses an enormous collection of material relating to the early
   days of the denomination, and key figures in its foundation and
   consolidation. It also holds Methodist newspapers and periodicals
   which can be useful for tracking down ministers' obituaries.
   Wesley Historical Society: wesleyhistoricalsociety.org.uk

Presbyterians

You can search the Protestant Dissenters' Registry via BMD
registers.co,uk/TheGenealogist. This served the congregations of
Baptists, Independents and Presbyterians in London and within
a 12-mile radius of the capital. However, parents from most parts
of the British Isles and even abroad also used the registry. It was
started in 1742, with retrospective entries going back to 1716, and
continued until 1837.

Presbyterian Historical Society of Ireland:
presbyterianhistoryireland.com
Presbyterian Historical Society: www.history.pcusa.org

Quakers

Quaker history begins with George Fox who established the Religious Society of Friends in the mid-seventeenth century. Members of the society became known as 'Quakers' because some of them trembled during religious experiences. Many Quakers faced persecution and many emigrated to North America.

There were four hierarchical levels of Quaker meetings and registers were originally kept by local or monthly meetings. From 1776 copies were also sent to the quarterly meeting (and these are now held at TNA). The registers were also recorded in 'digests', which contain much of the detail of the originals, and are often housed at local record offices and at Friends House – the Quaker headquarters in London. Important online sources available through TheGenealogist are the Quaker BMD registers held by TNA (series RG 6). They include registers, notes and certificates of births, marriages and burials from the years 1578 and 1841.

Quakers kept meticulous registers of births (Quakers did not practise baptism), marriages and deaths, as well as other records related to congregations. Register books began to be kept by Quaker meetings from the late 1650s, but in 1776 their whole registration system was overhauled. So post-1776 birth entries, for example, contain the date of birth, place of birth (locality, parish and county), parents' names (often with the father's occupation), the child's name and names of the witnesses.

Quakers' refusal to pay tithes led to them being subject to fines and even imprisonment. They were anxious to record these persecutions so books of sufferings were kept by monthly or quarterly meetings, and then recorded in the 'great book of sufferings' in London.

Library of the Religious Society of Friends: quaker.org.uk
Has details of the official Library of the Religious Society of
  Friends.
Quaker FHS: qfhs.co.uk
The Society website is very useful for getting to grips with unique
  Quaker records. Explains types of records such as minute books,
  membership lists and digests.
Quaker Archives, Leeds University Library:
library.leeds.ac.uk/special-collections
Comprise the Carlton Hill collection (broadly covering Leeds,
  Bradford, Settle and Knaresborough) and the Clifford Street
  collection (York and Thirsk areas, as well as Yorkshire-wide
  material).
Yorkshire Quaker Heritage Project:
www.hull.ac.uk/oldlib/archives/quaker/

REMEMBER

- As the refusal to bear arms is central to Quaker beliefs, you
  may be able to find references to Quakers in the records of
  Conscientious Objectors, held by TNA.
- Quakers, the Society of Friends, used the Julian Calendar up
  until March 1752, after which the vast majority of their
  records adopted the Gregorian Calendar. According to the
  Julian Calendar, the first day of the new year was 25 March
  'Lady Day', so a full year would run from 25 March to
  24 March.
- Roman Catholic registers were generally not kept before
  1778 and many of them are written in Latin. Catholic
  baptism registers will usually show the names of godparents.
- The Historic Chapels Trust site (www.hct.org.uk) hosts
  images and information about redundant chapels and places
  of worship.

FURTHER READING
Barratt, Nick. *Who Do You Think You Are? Encyclopedia of Genealogy*, Harper, 2008
Herber, Mark. *Ancestral Trails: The Complete Guide to British Genealogy and Family History*, The History Press, new edn 2005

WILLS AND PROBATE
Wills can reveal troubled relationships. Cardiff gent Miles Bassett put his pen to paper in the seventeenth century, leaving behind a document that is still preserved within the National Library of Wales' probate collection.

And [I could put] as little confidence in my crabbed churlish unnatural, heathenish, and unhuman sonne inlawe Leyson Evans and Anne his wife; I never found noe love, shame nor honestie with them. . . . but basenesse and falsehood, knaverie and deceipt in them all, ever unto me . . . they were my greatest Enemies, I had no comfort in anie of them, but trouble & sorrow ever, they sued me in Londone in the Exchequier and in the Comonplease, and in the Marches at Ludlowe, and in the greate Sessions at Cardiff and thus they have vexed me ever of a long time.

The 1627 will and inventory of carpenter Nicholas Perry of 'New Sarum' (Salisbury) describes how at a time of plague Perry took refuge in nearby Combe Bissett, and took the opportunity to make a nuncupative will (one dictated rather than written down). He made the will because his son Nicholas had threatened to 'use his wife hardly' and throw her out. So, Perry decided to give all his property to his younger son, Anthony. The associated inventory, not surprisingly, includes a lot of 'timber stuff'.

All this should hopefully encourage you to look into probate sources. Wills can not only offer you insights into a person's wealth and possessions, but also give a census-like snapshot of a household, with all kinds of relationships revealed, and, if there's an associate inventory, sometimes give you a virtual room by room tour of the house and belongings. In short, they can contain revealing information that is not available from any other source, and they stretch back to long before the census or civil registration. But they can also be hard to read, fragmentary, full of archaic and technical legalese, and, especially if there is no index or other finding aid, hard to track down.

Where there's wealth there's often a will, but not always, and lots of people of more modest means also left wills. Many left unproven wills to avoid legal fees, and even if your ancestor did not leave a will, they may have appeared in someone else's. According to the useful FamilySearch wiki on the subject of English probate material, it is estimated that 'courts probated estates (with or without a will) for fewer than 10 percent of English heads of households before 1858. However, as much as one-fourth of the population either left a will or was mentioned in one.' In Scotland, according to the National Records of Scotland guide to Wills and Testaments, even as late as 1961, only 'forty three per cent of Scots dying in that year left testamentary evidence of any sort'.

You should investigate what is online, as region to region, collection to collection this varies a great deal. Some archives have detailed research guides, indexes and even digitised material. Should you wish to know more about the aforementioned Miles Bassett, for example, you can explore the document via the National Library of Wales' wonderful database of free digital images of pre-1858 wills proved in Welsh ecclesiastical courts at www.llgc.org.uk/probate. And you can also view the allied inventory (ref: LL 1680-10) to see what they were all squabbling over.

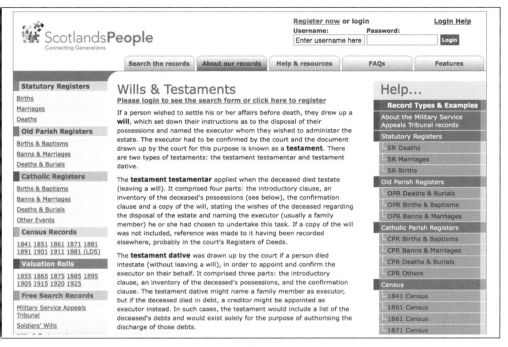

ScotlandsPeople
Connecting Generations

Search the records | About our records | Help & resources | FAQs | Features

Statutory Registers
Births
Marriages
Deaths

Old Parish Registers
Births & Baptisms
Banns & Marriages
Deaths & Burials

Catholic Registers
Births & Baptisms
Banns & Marriages
Deaths & Burials
Other Events

Census Records
1841 1851 1861 1871 1881
1891 1901 1911 1881 (LDS)

Valuation Rolls
1855 1865 1875 1885 1895
1905 1915 1920 1925

Free Search Records
Military Service Appeals
Tribunal
Soldiers' Wills

Wills & Testaments
Please login to see the search form or click here to register

If a person wished to settle his or her affairs before death, they drew up a **will**, which set down their instructions as to the disposal of their possessions and named the executor whom they wished to administer the estate. The executor had to be confirmed by the court and the document drawn up by the court for this purpose is known as a **testament**. There are two types of testaments: the testament testamentar and testament dative.

The **testament testamentar** applied when the deceased died testate (leaving a will). It comprised four parts: the introductory clause, an inventory of the deceased's possessions (see below), the confirmation clause and a copy of the will, stating the wishes of the deceased regarding the disposal of the estate and naming the executor (usually a family member) he or she had chosen to undertake this task. If a copy of the will was not included, reference was made to it having been recorded elsewhere, probably in the court's Registers of Deeds.

The **testament dative** was drawn up by the court if a person died intestate (without leaving a will), in order to appoint and confirm the executor on their behalf. It comprised three parts: the introductory clause, an inventory of the deceased's possessions, and the confirmation clause. The testament dative might name a family member as executor, but if the deceased died in debt, a creditor might be appointed as executor instead. In such cases, the testament would include a list of the deceased's debts and would exist solely for the purpose of authorising the discharge of those debts.

Help...

Record Types & Examples

About the Military Service
Appeals Tribunal records

Statutory Registers
└ SR Deaths
└ SR Marriages
└ SR Births

Old Parish Registers
└ OPR Deaths & Burials
└ OPR Births & Baptisms
└ OPR Banns & Marriages

Catholic Parish Registers
└ CPR Births & Baptisms
└ CPR Banns & Marriages
└ CPR Deaths & Burials
└ CPR Others

Census
└ 1841 Census
└ 1851 Census
└ 1861 Census
└ 1871 Census

Scottish testaments from between 1514 and 1925 have been digitised and copies are available through ScotlandsPeople.

Scottish Testaments

In Scotland 'testament' is the collective term for documents relating to wills and inventories. After a person died, if there was a will it would be taken to the sheriff courts to be confirmed, producing a document called a 'testament testamentar' (a grant of probate). If there was no will a 'testament dative' would be drawn up (a letter of administration) which would give power to executors to deal with the estate.

Testaments from between 1514 and 1925 have been digitised and copies are available through ScotlandsPeople, which also contains an index with over 611,000 index entries, each listing surname, forename, title, occupation and place of residence (where known) of the deceased person, the court in which the testament was recorded and the date. Index entries do not include names of executors, trustees, heirs to the estate, date of death or value of the estate.

Before 1823 testaments were recorded in the Commissary Court with jurisdiction over the parish in which the person died. And just as England's diocesan boundaries won't match ancient county boundaries, so these court boundaries, which roughly corresponded to medieval dioceses that existed before the Reformation in Scotland, bear no relation to county boundaries. Also, remember that the Edinburgh Commissary Court confirmed testaments for those who owned property in more than one area, and for Scots who died outside Scotland. And from 1824 Sheriff Courts took over responsibility for confirmation of testaments.

There are other sources online. Ancestry, for example, recently issued its National Probate Index – Calendar of Confirmations and Inventories between 1876 and 1936. The National Records of Scotland and ScotlandsPeople websites also have clear and concise guides to wills and testaments in Scotland (the latter going into more detail). In addition, you can view examples of will and associated documents from different areas.

Probate in England and Wales

There are lots of technicalities and idiosyncrasies to watch out for, but broadly speaking, prior to 1858, the situation in England and Wales was similar to pre-1824 Scotland in that the Church of England courts handled probate.

There were more than 300 Church probate courts set within a hierarchy – the higher court would handle the probate if the testator owned property in two or more areas. The lowest were the peculiar courts, which had jurisdiction over small areas. Next came archdeaconry courts (divisions within dioceses), bishops' courts (the highest diocesan courts), prerogative courts and the Prerogative Court of Canterbury – the highest court of all, used for wills of testators who died or owned property outside of England, foreigners who owned property in England, military personnel, persons having property in more than one probate jurisdiction and wealthier individuals.

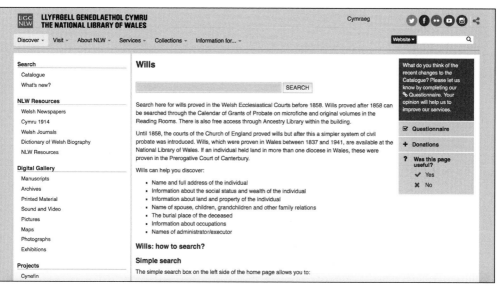

The National Library of Wales hosts a database of free digital images of pre-1858 wills proved in Welsh ecclesiastical courts at www.llgc.org.uk/probate.

So, to track down probate records you need to try to confirm the parish and year in which your ancestor died, then confirm which court (or courts) had jurisdiction. Then you can look for any surviving indexes and records.

The Nicholas Perry will quoted above, for example, comes from the diocese of Salisbury probate collection preserved at the Wiltshire & Swindon History Centre. However, this diocese is much bigger than the county of Wiltshire, meaning the collection also includes wills from Berkshire, Dorset and Devon, as well as Wiltshire. Indeed, the collection includes the 1680 will of Edward Wallis of 'Stoke next Guildford' in Surrey, describing him as being of an 'infirme and crazie body'.

From January 1858 the Principal Probate Registry, a network of civil courts called probate registries, replaced the ecclesiastical probate courts. And you can search the official government index to wills and administrations in England and Wales via the Probate Search website (probatesearch.service.gov.uk/#wills). This includes wills/administrations between 1858 and 1995 (and 1996 to

This facsimile of a 1468 deed was printed in 1876 insomnia cure Memorials of the Family of Scott, of Scot's Hall in the County of Kent, *by James Renat Scott.*

present), as well as an index to soldiers' wills (1850–1986), and there's the National Probate Calendar (1858–1966) available via Ancestry.

Irish Wills

Before a will can take effect a grant of probate must be made by a court. And if someone dies without a will, the court can grant letters of administration for the disposal of the estate. Since 1858 grants of probate and administration in Ireland have been made in the Principal and District Registries of the Probate Court (before 1877) or the High Court (after 1877). These are indexed in the calendars of wills and administrations that are held at the National Archives of Ireland. Up to 1917, the calendars cover the whole of Ireland. After 1918 they cover the twenty-six counties in the Republic while indexes covering the six counties of Northern Ireland are at PRONI. The National Archives of Ireland testamentary calendars can be searched online (1858–1920 and 1922–82).

Before 1858 grants of probate and administration were made by the courts of the Church of Ireland (the Prerogative Court and the Diocesan or Consistorial Courts). There are separate indexes of wills and administrations for each court and some indexes have been published – such as the Vicar's Index to Prerogative Wills, 1536–1810 and the Indexes to Dublin Grant Books and Wills, 1270–1800. Again, you can find more detail via the National Archives of Ireland research guides (nationalarchives.ie).

REMEMBER
- There's a natural assumption that only the more well-to-do left wills, but this is not always the case, and there's also a chance you may find references to your ancestor in other people's wills.
- The eldest son in family wills may not actually be mentioned, because he automatically inherited property of the deceased father.
- Technically, a will conveys immovable property to heirs and a testament conveys personal moveable property. But in general the term 'will' usually refers to both.
- A 'codicil' is a signed addition to a will.
- If someone dies 'intestate' (without leaving a will), then you

may find 'Letters of Administration'. This a document that appoints someone to preside over the distribution of the estate. There may also be a letter of administration attached to a will, if the named executor is deceased, unwilling or unable to act.

- Other potential probate sources you may come across include 'act books' (accounts of court actions) and 'bonds' (written guarantees that a person will perform tasks set by the probate court).
- Very few wills and probate documents survive before around 1400.
- Before 1882 a wife who died before her husband could not make a will except with her husband's consent or under a marriage settlement created before her marriage.
- Until 1858 the courts of the Church of England proved wills but after this a simpler system of civil probate was introduced.
- On 12 January 1858, the Court of Probate was established in London to prove all wills throughout England and Wales. Until 1870 most women did not make a will as they were not allowed officially to own any property. After 1870 a married woman could make a will and bequeath property settled upon her for her separate use, but only under certain specific circumstances.
- The Civil War disrupted the probate process as Parliament abolished ecclesiastical courts in 1653 (restored in 1661). Wills proved during this period are filed at the Prerogative Court of Canterbury.
- Before 1750 heirs often did not prove wills in order to avoid court costs. Some archives maintain collections of unproved wills.
- Starting in 1796, a tax or death duty was payable on many estates with a certain value. Read more about death or estate duty wills at nationalarchives.gov.uk/help-with-your-

research/research-guides/death-duties-1796-1903-further-research/.

- Until 1833 real property could be 'entailed'. This specified how property would be inherited in the future. An entail prevented subsequent inheritors from bequeathing the property to anyone except the heirs specified in the original entail.

ONLINE RESOURCES

Find a will: probatesearch.service.gov.uk/#wills

The official government probate search engine. Use this to find wills from January 1858 onwards proved in the Principal Probate Registry, a network of civil courts that replaced the ecclesiastical courts in England and Wales. A name and year of death is required to find wills, which should be ready for download within ten days of order – costing £10. Please note this was Beta testing at the time of writing so the above address may change.

FamilySearch wiki: familysearch.org/learn/wiki/en/Main_Page

FamilySearch wiki pages concentrating on individual counties often have links to probate records, detailing what survives where. In addition, you'll sometimes find links to probate collections that have been digitised and made available here – such as the Cheshire Probate Records, 1492–1940 collection at familysearch. org/search/collection/1589492.

The National Archives: nationalarchives.gov.uk/help-with-your-research/research-guides/wills-1384-1858/

You can search Discovery for records of Prerogative Court of Canterbury (PCC) wills in series PROB 11 (1384–1858). These are all registered copy wills – copies of the original probates written into volumes by clerks at the Church courts. Other TNA guides/collections include wills of Royal Navy and Royal Marines personnel (1786–1882) and county court death duty registers and famous wills (1552–1854).

National Archives of Ireland: nationalarchives.ie
Find out more about the National Archives of Ireland's probate collections. You can search Calendars of Wills and Administrations (1858–1922) and there's an online database of soldiers' wills (soldierswills.nationalarchives.ie), as well as a useful research guide with a glossary of legal terms.
ScotlandsPeople: scotlandspeople.gov.uk
Trawl the index to Scottish wills and testaments dating from 1513 to 1901 (listing surname, forename, title, occupation and place of residence), as well as the associated database of soldiers' wills.
National Library of Wales: llgc.org.uk
Explore 193,000 records of wills proved in the Welsh ecclesiastical courts prior to the introduction of civil probate in 1858. You can either search the entire index, or narrow down by individual courts.
Public Record Office of Northern Ireland:
www.proni.gov.uk/index/search_the_archives.htm
Details of all PRONI's online probate collections, including Will Calendars – a free index of wills from the district probate registries of Armagh, Belfast and Londonderry (1858–1943).
North East Inheritance Database:
familyrecords.dur.ac.uk/nei/data/
A database of pre-1858 probate records (wills and related documents) covering Northumberland and County Durham. Digital images of the original probate records (including wills and inventories, 1650–1857; copies of wills, 1527–1858; executors' and administration bonds, 1702–1858) are also available through FamilySearch.
The Gazette: www.thegazette.co.uk/wills-and-probate
Includes wills and probate notices printed in the London, Edinburgh and Belfast gazettes.
Ancestry: search.ancestry.co.uk/search/db.aspx?dbid=1904

Ancestry's probate collections include important National
  Probate Calendars.
TheGenealogist: thegenealogist.co.uk
  Diamond subscribers can enjoy several useful probate
  collections including many county wills indexes covering
  Yorkshire, Staffordshire, London, Leicestershire and more, as
  well as the PCC indexes and indexes to some Irish and Scottish
  wills.
Findmypast:
search.findmypast.co.uk/search-world-records/england-and-
wales-published-wills-and-probate-indexes-1300-1858
England & Wales Published Wills & Probate Indexes, 1300–1858.
Essex Wills: seax.essexcc.gov.uk
Search and access images of Essex probate material held at Essex
  Record Office.
Wiltshire Wills: www.wshc.eu/our-services/archives.html

FURTHER READING

Gibson, Jeremy and Else Churchill. *Probate Jurisdictions: Where
  to Look for Wills*, Federation of Family History Societies, 2002
  (for probate indexes produced since Gibson and Churchill's
  guide go towww.dur.ac.uk/a.r.millard/genealogy/probate.
  php)
Grannum, Karen and Nigel Taylor. *Wills and Probate Records:
  A Guide for Family Historians*, The National Archives, 2009

MIGRATION

In 1913 Joanna Archer had a child out of wedlock. The father was
Ishmael Cummings, a Sierra Leonean doctor and one of several
African professionals working at Newcastle's Royal Victoria
Infirmary, where Joanna was junior matron. Their son, Ivor
Cummings, would grow up in Addiscombe, south London, where

he suffered prejudice because of the colour of his skin – on one occasion fellow pupils at Whitgift School setting light to his curly hair.

Ivor wished to become a doctor, but social barriers of the time were such that he abandoned those dreams, instead forging a career as a civil servant, becoming a well-known figure in London's black community. He was working as a civil servant in the Colonial Office when early one morning in June 1948 he was sent to Tilbury Docks. He was there to meet an initial shipload of Jamaicans who were arriving in Britain for the first time aboard the *Empire Windrush*.

The arrival of the *Windrush* is a watershed moment in the history of migration to Britain. It wasn't some obscure event that has since been given greater significance by historians. The day before the ship arrived the London *Evening Standard* sent out an aeroplane from Croydon Aerodrome to photograph the vessel as she approached. The image and news of the approaching migrants made the front page under the headline: 'Welcome Home! Evening Standard 'plane greets 400 sons of Empire'.

'From the air,' wrote *Standard* reporter Denise Richards, 'the *Empire Windrush* was little different from many of the ships which sail daily, but to four hundred people on board she was the beginning of a new life. . . . The airplane circled for fifteen minutes, and gradually apprehension turned to joy as the passengers realised they were receiving their first welcome to England.'

The *Windrush* had set off from Kingston, Jamaica on Empire Day, 1948. The majority of the migrants paid £28 to travel to Great Britain, responding to job advertisements that had appeared in local newspapers. Britain was suffering from major post-war labour shortages, and the passenger lists from that first arrival record an array of occupations – welder, carpenter, mechanic, painter, tailor, bookkeeper, farmer and fitter. To begin with many settlers were housed in a deep air raid shelter in Clapham

Imperial Direct West India Mail Service Co., Ltd.,
ELDER, DEMPSTER & CO.

'The bridge' that carried you over.

*Yours very sincerely
W. R. Rowe*

One of the Imperial Mail Liners in Avonmouth Dock.

Souvenir postcards of a sea voyage. This one records RMS Port Royal's run from Kingston to Bristol, captained by W.R. Rowe.

SOUVENIR.

R.M.S. "PORT ROYAL."   Voyage 29

Kingston to Bristol

Captain—W. R. ROWE.

Chief Officer,   Doctor
A. C. SELFE   E. W. LYNCH

Chief Engineer.—R. MARSHALL.

Steward-in-charge—G. A. TOVEY.

DAILY RUNS.

		Knots
Sept.29 Sailed	...	
30	...	250
1	...	312
2	...	315
3	...	326
4	...	317
5	...	308
6	...	329
7	...	335
8	...	331
9	...	333
10	...	340
11	...	300
Distance to run	...	223
Total	...	4019

Common, many eventually settling in nearby Brixton as this was the location of the nearest labour exchange.

The arrival of the *Windrush* is just one chapter in the story of migration in and out of the British Isles and Ireland. Other chapters include the Huguenots, members of the French Protestant Church who left their homes in France to escape religious persecution; there was the forced displacement of the Highland Clearances; and the mass starvation, disease and emigration of the Great Hunger in Ireland.

Trade pulled individuals and families across country borders, from the nineteenth-century Irish navvies who helped build Britain's railways to employees of the Hudson Bay Company. The East India Company played a vital role in British expansion and control overseas, for hundreds of years employing thousands of traders, administrators, politicians, sailors and soldiers. There were also the 'assisted' migrations, such as the Home Children of the later Victorian period, or the Highlands & Islands Emigration Society, which assisted almost 5,000 individuals to leave western Scotland for Australia between 1852 and 1857. And there were forced migrations, the thousands of criminals transported firstly to North America and later to Australia.

Migration sources are complex. To keep things simple, I will first look at records of migrants entering the British Isles, before turning to records of those moving elsewhere.

Incoming

TNA's guide to immigration research begins by warning the reader that tracing immigrants can be difficult because many records held there are incomplete, in addition to the fact that some record series only cover certain periods or types of immigrant.

In general, surviving records refer to aliens (a non-citizen of the parent country), 'denizens' (a permanent resident, but not a citizen) and the process of naturalisation – when someone from outside the country becomes a legal citizen.

The earliest TNA sources that may potentially include references to foreign subjects and aliens include Chancery records, records of the Exchequer and state papers. Some early lists of people mentioned in the Calendar of State Papers, Domestic (1537–1625) can be searched via British History Online (british-history.ac.uk). Another source is Parliament or patent rolls which contain records of acts of naturalisation and grants of denizations. There are also Treasury in-letters, which contain references to refugees and other foreign people who received annuities, pensions and other payments in return for services rendered to the Crown. (There are indexes to the Calendar of Treasury Papers between 1556 and 1745.)

A great online resource for people researching in this early period is the England's Immigrants Database at englands immigrants.com. This is a fully searchable database containing over 64,000 names of people known to have migrated to England between 1330 and 1550 – covering the Hundred Years War, the Black Death, the Wars of the Roses and the Reformation.

The situation simplifies after 1793. Mass migration during this period (caused largely by the French Revolution and Napoleonic Wars) led to the passing of the Aliens Act of 1793. From then all arriving migrants had to register with the Justice of Peace, providing personal information, which would then be passed to the Aliens Office. The original Aliens Office certificates have not survived (although some indexes have), but original Justice of Peace records relating to arrivals may survive locally at county record offices – normally among quarter sessions material. Hull History Centre, for example, has certificates of arrival of aliens issued at the port between 1793 and 1815.

A second Aliens Act was passed in 1836. Now newly arrived migrants had to sign a certificate of arrival, and these certificates, for arrivals to England and Scotland, are held at TNA in series HO 2. The certificates should record nationality, profession, date of arrival, last country visited and other details. Through Ancestry, thanks to its partnership with TNA, you can search Alien Arrivals (1810–11 and 1826–69) and Aliens' registration cards (1918–57) covering the London area only.

Another useful and accessible source is not part of migration records as such, but registers kept by settled communities. The non-parochial registers contained within RG 4 and RG 8 at TNA date from the sixteenth to twentieth centuries and are records kept by the French, Dutch, German and Swiss churches in London and elsewhere. These can be searched via BMDregisters. co.uk.

Other important TNA collections include: naturalisation case papers (1789–1934), which can be searched via Discovery;

The National Archives' immigration guide leads to all kinds of useful online resources.

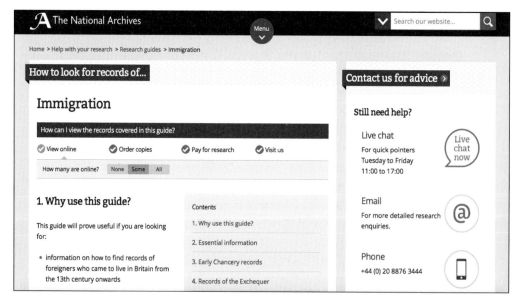

incoming passenger lists (1878–1960, held in BT 26), documenting people arriving from countries outside Europe and the Mediterranean area, available via Ancestry. The latter include details such as name, date of birth and age, ports of departure and arrival, and details of the vessel. Although remember that many of the pre-1890 lists were irregularly destroyed by the Board of Trade. Also available via Ancestry are the naturalisation certificates and declarations of British nationality (1870–1912). These will usually list the immigrant's name, residence, birthplace, age, parents' names, name of spouse (if married), occupation and children (if still of dependent age).

Thanks partly to post-war labour shortages between the years 1948 and 1962 there were no restrictions on immigrants from Commonwealth countries, and the British Nationality Act of 1948 made it relatively simple for migrants to obtain citizenship. Certificates of citizenship issued by the Home Office from this period have also survived and can be found at TNA in HO 334.

Outgoing

Before you start your research into a migrant leaving the UK and Ireland, it's useful to have the name of the ship they travelled on, and the ports of departure and arrival. This is easier said than done and while there are some online resources that can help you find this information, coverage is patchy.

Findmypast, through partnership with TNA, boasts outward passenger lists between 1890 and 1960. These were lists from both UK and Irish ports, recording those travelling to the USA, Canada, India, New Zealand and Australia.

Other important collections include Foreign Office records, such as passport registers and indexes, or, for researching individuals who migrated (or were transported) to Australia, there are the New South Wales original correspondence, entry books and registers (between 1784 and 1900). These contain lists of names of emigrants, settlers and convicts. The website of The National Archives of Australia has more information about emigration to Australia. In addition, details of some 8.9 million free settlers to New South Wales, 1826–1922 can be searched and downloaded online at ancestry.com.au, for a fee. Other Antipodean sources include registers of cabin passengers emigrating to New Zealand (1839–50).

TNA has original correspondence and entry books (1814–71), which can be explored via Discovery, and Land and Emigration Commission papers (1840–94), which include registers of births and deaths of emigrants at sea from 1854 to 1869, lists of ships chartered from 1847 to 1875 and registers of surgeons appointed from 1854 to 1894. You can also search Discovery by name for case histories of all those evacuated by the Children's Overseas Reception Board during the Second World War.

Another common area of research is child migration. According to TNA, it is estimated that between 1618 and 1967 about 150,000 children were sent to the British colonies and dominions as part of various schemes, mainly to America, Canada and Australia, but also Zimbabwe (Rhodesia), New Zealand, South Africa and the Caribbean. 'Many of the children were in the care of the voluntary organisations who arranged for their migration. Child emigration peaked from the 1870s until 1914 – about 80,000 children were sent to Canada alone during this period.' (http://www.nationalarchives.gov.uk/help-with-your-research/research-guides/emigration/).

The Poor Law Amendment Act of 1850 allowed Boards of Guardians to send children under 16 overseas. But any records of specific cases are most likely to survive within records held in local archives. Aberdeen City and Aberdeenshire Archives' Poor Law material includes the General Registers of the Poor for Peterhead. One entry concerns 4-year-old Elspet Niddrie, whose dying mother and adult half-sister were unable to care for her. The council decided she should be sent to her aunt, Jane Lemmon (née Niddrie) who had emigrated to America in 1904. The case ends with the Inspector of the Poor writing: 'Passage paid to Boston USA and sent to Aunt . . . sailed today on Allan Liner *Numidian*'. (Elspet lived in Massachusetts, went on to marry a bus driver, had four children and died in December 1983.)

There are TNA-held Colonial Office reports on pauper child emigrants resident in Canada (1887–92). These comment on condition, health, character, schooling and church attendance of each child, as well as the children's own view of their new homes. They also record the union or parish from which they were sent, as well as each child's name, age and host's name and address. Remember too that useful information may reside in records of initiatives held by the likes of Dr Barnardo's Homes, the Overseas Migration Board and the Big Brother emigration scheme.

Away from economic and assisted migrants, there were thousands of forced migrants – namely criminals transported first to North America and later to Australia. This began in 1615, when criminals were first shipped to America or the West Indies, often sent to work on plantations. It is estimated that more than 50,000 English men, women and children were sentenced, crimes ranging from the theft of a handkerchief to highway robbery. One important source for this period is Peter Coldham's landmark work *The Complete Book of Emigrants in Bondage* (and via Ancestry you can also access *More Emigrants in Bondage, 1614–1775).*

After the American Revolution in 1776 convicts had to be sent elsewhere and the first convict ships, known as the First Fleet, arrived in Australia in January 1788. The flow of convicted transportees finally slowed during the 1850s and ceased altogether when the system was abolished in 1868. While the records for this period of transportation are fractured, there are lots of websites with data and information about the history of transportation and how to research individuals. Amateur site Convicts to Australia (members.iinet.net.au/~perthdps/convicts/) has lots of advice, as well as transcribed lists of the First, Second

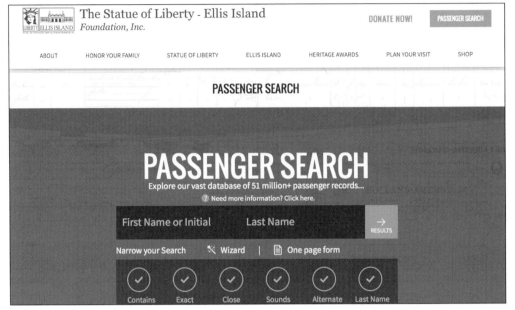

The wonderful Ellis Island Foundation website, where you can trawl a vast database of more than 51 million passenger records.

and Third Fleets. The National Archives of Ireland has an online database of Irish convicts transported to Australia, compiled from transportation registers and petitions to government for pardon or commutation of sentence. The wonderful Proceedings of the Old Bailey London 1674–1834 website (oldbaileyonline.org) can be searched by punishment – go to the advanced search and select 'Transportation'. Also, Australian state records include those of New South Wales's Convict Indexes to Certificates of Freedom (1823–69).

These are just some of a vast array of potential sources that may survive. But of course the next step is tracking any record of your ancestor's arrival in their new home. For this you will need to contact and explore archives overseas. For migration to the USA, for example, there is the likes of the Ellis Island Foundation, which grants access to vast databases of arriving migrants processed at the famous Ellis Island station.

Remember to look out for societies and organisations that focus on your area of interest. The Families In British India Society (fibis.org) has an immense and very useful Wiki, with all kinds of useful advice and data for tracing family members overseas. While the Immigrant Ships Transcribers Guild (immigrantships.net) offers transcribed passenger lists that can be searched by port of arrival or departure. British Home Children in Canada (canadian britishhomechildren.weebly.com) has data relating to approximately 118,000 children sent to Canada from the UK under the Child Immigration scheme (1863–1939).

An important website for Irish migration research is Documenting Ireland: Parliament, People & Migration (www.dippam.ac.uk). This is a family of sites that together document Irish migration since the eighteenth century. It includes the 'Irish Emigration Database', based on roughly 33,000 documents – including letters, diaries and journals written by migrants, and newspaper material such as advertisements and overseas BMD notices. This really is a fascinating website, where you can spend many hours reading first-hand accounts of individuals starting new lives overseas.

ONLINE RESOURCES

The Ships List: theshipslist.com
Includes passenger lists from across the globe.
Immigrant Ships Transcribers Guild: immigrantships.net
Transcribed passenger lists that can be searched by port of arrival or departure.
East India Company Ships: eicships.info/index.html
Information on ships and voyages of the East India Company's mercantile service.
The National Archives: nationalarchives.gov.uk
There are several research guides to immigration, emigration,

---

travel and relating to specific categories of records, such as naturalisation and passports.

On Their Own, Britain's Child Migrants: otoweb.cloudapp.net

Child migrants to Canada, Australia and other Commonwealth countries from the 1860s to the 1960s.

England's Immigrants Database: englandsimmigrants.com

Findmypast: findmypast.co.uk

Some important collections include Passenger Lists leaving UK (1890–1960) and Index to Register of Passport Applications (1851–1903) collections.

Ancestry: ancestry.co.uk

Has Alien Arrivals (1810–11, 1826–69), Incoming passenger lists (1878–1960), Outgoing passenger lists (1890–1960) and Aliens Entry Books (1794–1921).

TheGenealogist: thegenealogist.co.uk

Immigration/emigration collections include passenger lists and naturalisation records.

BMDregisters: bmdregisters.co.uk

Search for births, marriages and deaths on British registered ships and non-parochial registers from French, Dutch, German and Swiss churches.

British Settlers in Argentina and Uruguay: argbrit.org

London Metropolitan Archives: www.cityoflondon.gov.uk/things-to-do/london-metropolitan-archives/Pages/default.aspx

Holds an array of resources relating to migration to London, including records for black and Asian, Irish and French migrants.

Scottish Emigration Database: abdn.ac.uk/emigration/

Records of passengers who embarked from Scottish ports between 1890 and 1960.

The Highland Clearances: highlandclearances.co.uk

Black Cultural Archives: bcaheritage.org.uk

Child Migrants Trust: childmigrantstrust.com

Black Presence in Britain: blackpresence.co.uk

India Office Family Search, British Library: indiafamily.bl.uk/UI/
National Maritime Museum: rmg.co.uk
Jewish Genealogical Society of Great Britain: jgsgb.org.uk
Huguenot Society: huguenotsociety.org.uk
Families In British India Society: fibis.org
Home to lots of advice for tracing family members overseas, as well as a database of nearly 1,500,000 names and the expanding Fibiwiki at wiki.fibis.org/index.php/Main_Page.
Anglo-German Family History Society: agfhs.org.uk

Ireland
The National Archives of Ireland: nationalarchives.ie
Documenting Ireland, Parliament, People & Migration: dippam.ac.uk
Family of sites that draws on sources relating to Irish migration and maintains the Irish Emigration Database of letters, diaries and journals written by migrants, as well as newspaper material.
The Mellon Centre for Migration Studies, Ulster American Folk Park: www.qub.ac.uk/cms/

Canada
British Home Children in Canada: canadianbritishhomechildren.weebly.com
Library & Archives Canada: bac-lac.gc.ca/eng
Hudson Bay Company Heritage: www.hbcheritage.ca

America
Ellis Island: libertyellisfoundation.org
Explore the vast database of 51 million+ passenger records as well as the Immigrant Wall of Honor, a permanent exhibit of individual and family names.
Castle Garden: castlegarden.org
The pre-Ellis Island immigrant centre, Castle Garden. This provides a database of 11,000,000 names (1820–92).

US Immigrant Ancestors Project: immigrants.byu.edu
Uses emigration registers to locate information about the
   birthplaces of immigrants.
The National Archives of America: archives.gov

Australia and New Zealand
National Archives of Australia: naa.giv.au
Archives New Zealand: archives.govt.nz
Migration Heritage Australia: migrationheritage.nsw.gov.au
Convicts to Australia: members.iinet.net.au/~perthdps/convicts/
Free databases relating to transportation to Australia, including
   transcribed lists of the First, Second and Third Fleets.

Slavery
Legacies of British Slave-ownership: ucl.ac.uk/lbs
Trans-Atlantic Slave Trade Database: slavevoyages.org
Recovered Histories: recoveredhistories.org
Digitised eighteenth- and nineteenth-century literature on the
   transatlantic slave trade.
Wilberforce Institute for the study of Slavery and Emancipation:
   www2.hull.ac.uk/fass/wise/about_us.aspx
Global Slavery Index: globalslaveryindex.org
My Slave Ancestors: myslaveancestors.com

REMEMBER
- The last known denization was granted in 1873.
- In 1905 a new Aliens Act meant that aliens could only enter
  the UK at the discretion of the authorities. After 1919 they
  had to register with the local police.
- The main TNA record series containing information about
  emigrants and emigration policy are Colonial Office (CO),
  Home Office (HO), Board of Trade (BT) and Treasury (T).

- If you're reading about migration you may begin to notice that anything good is the work of 'settlers' and 'pioneers', anything bad is down to 'the British'!
- In June 1940 the Children's Overseas Reception Board was set up to administer offers from Canada, Australia, New Zealand, South Africa and the USA to care for British children in private homes.
- Evacuation stopped on 17 September 1940 when the SS *City of Benares* was torpedoed with the loss of seventy-seven children bound for Canada.
- TNA's Discovery catalogue also lists overseas repositories (discovery.nationalarchives.gov.uk/find-an-archive). Below the map of the UK you can browse by country name. It usually lists the main national archive and/or library.

FURTHER READING

Barratt, Nick. *Who Do You Think You Are? Encyclopedia of Genealogy*, Harper, 2008

Kershaw, Roger. *Migration Records: A Guide for Family Historians*, The National Archives, 2009

THOSE WHO SERVED: A MILITARY MISCELLANY

It is common to stumble upon evidence of military service in family archives, from certificates, buttons, caps, uniforms, medals and photographs to the more ephemeral stuff of family legend. My father still dines out on memories of national service: arriving as a fresh-faced youth and being mercilessly taunted for his posh accent. His old army box, labelled in chipped black paint with his rank and regiment, held my toys as a child, and, when I briefly took up coarse fishing, my weights and tackle lived in his khaki army bag.

Step back a generation, and the catalogue to the reel to reel tape collection of my paternal grandfather – full of old Goon Shows and classical radio broadcasts from the 1960s – is neatly noted down in an old Royal Air Force Signal Office Diary, the columns for 'Watch Times', 'Remarks' and 'Signatures' taken up with details of conductors, soloists and broadcast dates. The same grandfather was a carpenter and tinkerer, and I still play his home-made, box-shaped ukulele, constructed from whatever he could find during wartime service in Africa. My maternal grandfather served with the

'He died for freedom and honour'. The memorial plaque for Kenneth Richard Scott.

Royal Artillery during the Second World War. He helpfully left a modest home-bound volume of typed wartime memories, including tales of his faithful old dog Gunner Jones and his occasional association with flying ace Douglas Bader (my grandfather, not the dog).

Indeed, traces of both world wars pepper the walls and bookshelves of my parents' house. Stumble over the poorly trained spaniel into their smoke-damaged kitchen, and near a wooden owl of my own construction, a painting of hands by middle-sister Kate and a sculpted clay boot by eldest sister Annabel lies a Memorial Plaque. These were issued after the First World War to the next of kin of all British and Empire service personnel killed as a result of the war. The plaques were made of bronze and became popularly known as 'Dead Man's Penny'. Explore the bookshelves nearby and with perseverance you will find the name of the same individual, noted down in a wonderful book of signatures compiled at a birthday ball in the early 1900s.

Let's end our brief tour in the downstairs loo. Here, on the wall next to the throne and the guitar that can't be tuned, is a picture of what appears to be a military inspection. In fact, it's the future King George VI being shown a neat row of Barnardo's children by my great-great-grandfather Sir William Fry. And just along we have a telegram from King Edward VIII (the one who abdicated), congratulating the same great-great-grandfather on his diamond wedding.

All this is meant to serve as an illustration of the kind of clues that may survive in your own archive. From the disparate items above, I can all but confirm my father's rank and regiment, I can deduce that one grandfather served in the RAF and I have the

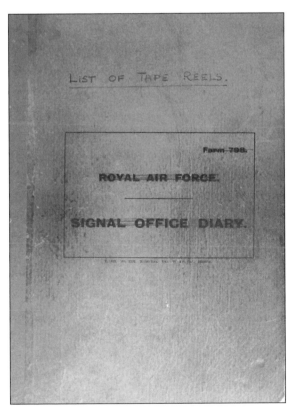

This Royal Air Force Signal Office Diary was commandeered by my paternal grandfather to catalogue his reel to reel tape recordings.

name of another relation who lost his life in the First World War. As a starting point, it's not bad. And if you combine all that with the ability to question living relatives, you may well have amassed a good amount of hearsay and more concrete information before you even start delving into official military sources and datasets.

There are plenty of bigger and better books that focus solely on military research for genealogists, or specific periods and conflicts. My aim here is quickly and efficiently to lay out some important facts about the military, list the main twentieth-century collections and draw attention to some of the best and most useful online resources for carrying out research remotely, for learning more about regiments, uniforms, campaign medals and more. The subject is in a sense 'simple' as so many important collections are preserved at TNA in Kew. But, in reality, it is rather complicated. With any military research it's important to try to ascertain when the individual joined.

The Navy
- The Royal Navy is traditionally the oldest part of the British armed forces, founded during the reign of Henry VIII, and so is known as the 'Senior Service'.
- The navy divided its men into ratings, the name used for ordinary seaman, and officers. How much information was recorded changed over time, so an important piece of information to try to confirm is when the individual joined.
- Tracing ratings before 1853 can be difficult. One useful free tool is the Trafalgar Ancestors database (nationalarchives.gov.uk/trafalgarancestors/) which lists all those who fought in Nelson's fleet at the Battle of Trafalgar on 21 October 1805.
- Ships' muster and pay books (1667–1878) were essentially crew lists, and are the likeliest place to find references to ratings before 1853. You can search TNA's Discovery catalogue for muster/pay books from a particular ship.

- Ratings records after 1853 become more detailed. The Royal Navy ratings' service records (1853–1928) collection is available online via TNA's website. This comprises more than 700,000 Royal Navy service records for ratings, drawn from continuous service engagement books, registers of seamen's service and continuous record cards.
- Records of servicemen who joined after 1923 are still held by the navy. Next of kin can request a summary of a service record for an individual who joined after May 1917 from the Ministry of Defence.
- A commissioned officer was someone who became an officer by being awarded a royal commission, usually after passing an examination. These are different from warrant officers. Commissioned officers include admirals, commodores, captains, commanders and lieutenants. Warrant officers include gunners, boatswains, carpenters, ropemakers, chaplains, surgeons and engineers.
- Most nineteenth-century service records include officer's name and rank, ships they served in as well as dates of entry/discharge from each vessel. Records can also include date of death, birth and next of kin.
- Royal Navy officers' service records 1756–1931 are online. From series ADM 196, they include records for commissioned officers joining the navy up to 1917 and warrant officers joining up to 1931. You can search for free via Discovery and download for a fee. You can also search officers' service record cards and files (*c.* 1880–1950s) and Ancestry has a Commissioned Sea Officers of the Royal Navy database.
- Ancestry has Royal Navy campaign, long service and good conduct medals – this collection includes First World War and Second World War medal and award rolls. Remember, digital microfilm copies of these records are also available to download from TNA free of charge.

- For officers you can also try Navy Lists – official published quarterly lists recording Royal Navy officers on active duty. These include rank, seniority and the ship or establishment in which the officer was serving. These are available from a number of websites, including archive.org (free of charge).

The Army

- Just as navy sources for ratings and officers can be found in different places, so there are different sources for army soldiers and officers. Soldier ranks include Private, Lance Corporal, Corporal, Sergeant and Warrant Officer. Officer ranks include Lieutenant, Captain, Major, Colonel, Brigadier and General.
- Always remember that many First World War files were lost or damaged by bombing in 1940.
- With army research it's important to identify the individual's military unit. If the soldier died during the world wars you can find this through the Commonwealth War Graves Commission website (cwgc.org).
- Potential army career sources include service records, casualty information, medal records and unit/operational histories. Most service records for soldiers discharged after the beginning of the First World War are with TNA, but some are held by the Ministry of Defence. Army service records for the Second World War are still with the Ministry of Defence. It does have other sources relating to the Second World War, including army casualty lists (in WO 417) which cover officers, other ranks and nurses.
- Findmypast's important army collections include British Army Service Records (1760–1915), containing records of more than 2 million soldiers. These include ordinary soldiers and officers and were drawn from militia service records, Chelsea Pensioners service' and discharge records, and Boer War soldiers' documents from the Imperial Yeomanry. The

If you're missing documentary evidence of an ancestor's military career, any photographs showing uniform, cap badges or medals can provide vital clues.

site also has the 1914–20 Service Records collection, drawn from WO 363 service records and WO 364 pension records.

- Ancestry's army collections, also in partnership with TNA, include First World War service Records, pension records and medal rolls. Also, there's the Military Campaign Medal and Award Rolls (1793–1949) database, which contains lists of more than 2.3 million officers, enlisted personnel and other individuals entitled to medals and awards – although this particular dataset **does not** include First World War or Second World War medal and award rolls.
- You can search for officers' service records (1914–22) through TNA's catalogue. Also, for a fee, you can search campaign medal index cards (1914–20).
- Published Army Lists can also be used to trace officers' careers. These were published monthly, quarterly and half-yearly. They list active officers and contain details of promotions.

The Royal Air Force
- Records of airmen and officers of the RAF are kept in different places depending on when they served. You can also search some RAF service records via TNA's Discovery catalogue for free. Individual image downloads cost £3.30.
- The RAF was formed in April 1918 when the Royal Flying Corps (RFC) and Royal Naval Air Service (RNAS) were amalgamated. TNA's guide to RAF personnel notes that 'someone who served in the RFC or RNAS as well as the RAF may have service records in more than one place'. There are also research guides dedicated to both RFC officers/airmen and RNAS officers/ratings, and the Women's Royal Air Force (WRAF).
- The RNAS was formed in 1914. You can search and download records of men who served between 1914 and 1918 via nationalarchives.gov.uk/help-with-your-

research/research-guides/royal-naval-air-service-officers-service-records-1906-1918/.

- RAF airmen service records (not officers) between 1912 and 1939 are available on Findmypast. These include details of date/place of birth, physical description, next of kin, promotions, units and medals. The record set contains records of almost 343,000 airmen.
- Findmypast also has officer service records (1912–20), containing records of 101,266 officers, and the RAF 1918 muster roll. The former boasts records of Nobel Prize-winning author William Faulkner and W.E. Johns, creator of the fictional flying ace 'Biggles'.
- The Battle of Britain Memorial website (battleofbritainmemorial.org) includes a database of all those who were awarded the Battle of Britain clasp.

Regimental and County Collections

There were various systems for mustering local forces before a Militia Act of 1757 established formal militia regiments across England and Wales. These were essentially part-time voluntary forces, organised by county and the records of conscription (between 1758 and 1831) serve as a kind of census as every year each parish was supposed to draw up lists of adult males, before holding a ballot to choose who would serve. TNA has a research guide focusing on militia, and the original lists, where they survive, are often at county archives or regimental archives. It's also worth checking what the family history society in your area of interest has produced – you'll often find they have published transcribed militia lists.

Many regiments look after their own collections and museums. These archives, usually accessible by appointment, may be maintained at the museum itself, or may have been deposited at the local county record office.

Even if no official regimental archive has been deposited,

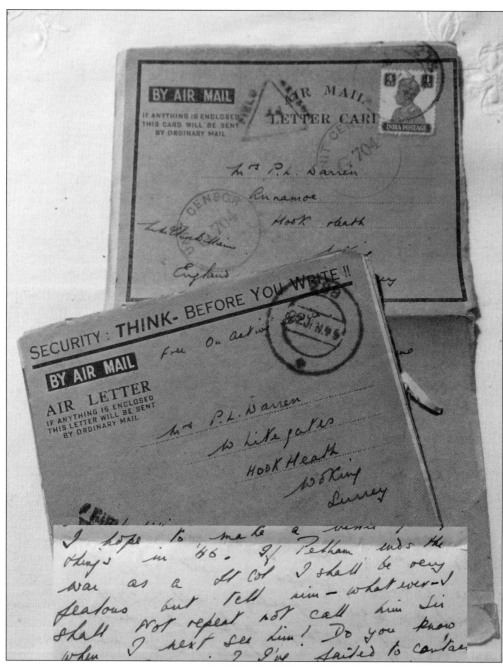

'Security: Think – Before You Write!!' These wartime letters contain a useful piece of information – that a relation may have ended the war with the rank of Lieutenant Colonel.

county archives will almost certainly have some kind of material relating to local military history. The North Yorkshire County Record Office has complete transcripts of returns of men enrolled to serve in the navy *c.* 1795. These relate to various North Riding wapentakes, but include men originating from all over the country. The Surrey History Centre in Woking shelters the vast Queen's Royal Surrey Regiment archive, spanning four centuries and 45m of shelving, comprising battalion war diaries, private journals, official photograph albums and even recordings of veterans' reminiscences.

The museum and archives of the Prince of Wales's Own Regiment of Yorkshire has unique historical artefacts such as the Amherst Flag, flown above the Citadel at Quebec after the Victory of the British Army led by Lord Amherst, to more practical genealogical sources such as enlistment registers, war diaries (including that of the 15th Leeds Pals Battalion, covering the first day of the Somme), photographs, personal diaries and correspondence (including the letter informing the next of kin that Private Johnson of 2nd Battalion, East Yorkshire Regiment, was listed as missing).

The Green Howards Regimental Museum, also in North Yorkshire, has regimental enlistment registers, detailing campaigns, wounds, medals and rewards as well as rank, 'character' and cause of discharge. And they have the 19th Foot regimental register of marriages and baptisms (1839–50) and a Yorkshire Regiment Punishment Book (1878–89), showing the record of a private sentenced to imprisonment and hard labour for fraudulent enlistment.

Ephemeral highlights from the Gordon Highlanders Museum in Aberdeen include a postcard sent home from a Japanese POW camp by Lance Corporal Bill Angus, 2nd Battalion, The Gordon Highlanders. The entire 2nd Battalion was captured when Singapore fell to Japanese forces in February 1942. Bill was wounded by shrapnel during the battle and sent to work on the

'Death Railway' in Thailand. In addition, they hold the VC awarded to Captain Sir Ernest Beachcroft Beckwith Towse for two separate actions in the Boer War, the second of which blinded him.

These are just a few random examples of what can reside in regimental collections. To see if there are any that might hold information relating to your ancestor's military career, try the Army Museums website (armymuseums.org.uk). Some museum websites have details of collections and archives, online finding aids and offer research services. Others are a bit more spartan. A great example is the website of the Royal Leicestershire Regiment (royal leicestershireregiment.org.uk), a wonderful digitised regimental archive, where you can search through over 65,000 soldier records dating back to 1688, read associated medals awards and citations, and explore digital copies of regimental journals.

ONLINE RESOURCES
Subscription
Ancestry: ancestry.co.uk/military

Home to several important TNA collections such as Army Service Records (1914–20) and Naval Officer and Rating Service Records (1802–1919).

Findmypast: search.findmypast.co.uk/search-united-kingdom-records-in-military-armed-forces-and-conflict

Boasts over 12,500,000 British records relating to military service, including Royal Navy & Marine Service Records (1899–1919) and the Royal Navy Officers Medal Roll (1914–20).

Forces War Records: forces-war-records.co.uk

Specialist subscription site which has all kinds of army material that you can explore by conflict/era. Has data relating to the Royal Naval College in Dartmouth, Royal Marines and Royal Navy Officers' Campaign Medal Rolls (1914–20), and a

database of Royal Navy/Royal Marines recipients of the 1914
Star Medal. Datasets include RAF Formations List, 1918,
Fighter Command Losses, 1940 and Aviators Certificates,
1905–26.

TheGenealogist: thegenealogist.co.uk
Military material includes First World War casualty lists – drawn
from weekly/daily War Office lists – and a POW database.

Free

Age of Nelson: ageofnelson.org
Hosts two useful databases – Royal Navy officers in the French
Revolutionary and Napoleonic wars (1793–1815), and the
seamen and marines who fought at the Battle of Trafalgar in
1805.

Anglo-Afghan War: garenewing.co.uk/angloafghanwar/
History of the Second Anglo-Afghan War (1878–80).

Army Museums: armymuseums.org.uk/ancestor.htm
Register of museums and a general introduction to researching
army ancestors.

Australian War Memorial: awm.gov.au
Includes all kinds of material relating to the Australian
experience of war, including centenary digitisation project
ANZAC Connections and details of personnel serving in pre-
First World War conflicts.

Battle of Britain Memorial: battleofbritainmemorial.org

Boer War Roll of Honour: roll-of-honour.com/Boer/
This page details the scope of the Boer Roll of Honour
database. The right-hand column leads to details of UK Boer
War memorials.

Bomber Command: rafbombercommand.com
History of RAF bomber aircrews, airmen and airwomen during
the Second World War.

Bomber History: bomberhistory.co.uk
Has sections telling the stories of 49 Squadron, as well as

specific raids and air attacks on British soil.

Britain's Small Forgotten Wars: britainssmallwars.co.uk

British Battles: britishbattles.com

Has a number of pages covering battles from the period including details of casualties and uniforms.

British Medals Forum: britishmedalforum.com

Covers British, Canadian, Australian, New Zealand, Indian, South African and all Commonwealth medals.

Commonwealth War Graves Commission: cwgc.org

Searchable database of the 1,700,000 service personnel who died during the two world wars.

Cross & Cockade International: www.crossandcockade.com

The First World War Aviation Historical Society.

Europeana 1914–1918: europeana1914-1918.eu/

Explore letters, diaries, photographs, films, documents and more through this European-wide project.

Fleet Air Arm Archive: fleetairarmarchive.net

Has a Debt of Honour Register, POW database and biographies of decorated officers.

The Gazette: thegazette.co.uk

Officers' commissions, promotions and appointments were published in the London *Gazette*. You can also search and browse military awards from MiDs (mentioned in despatches) to the Victoria Cross.

Great War Forum: 1914-1918.invisionzone.com/

Forum dedicated to First World War military research.

History of RAF: rafweb.org

Imperial War Museums, Research: iwm.org.uk/research

Includes guides to tracing individuals from the army, Royal Flying Corps, RAF, Royal Navy and Merchant Navy, POWs and those involved in the home front. It's been given a real tablet/smartphone makeover of late, with lots of blog-style articles on all kinds of subjects – including the Next of Kin Memorial Plaque (or Dead Man's Penny) at iwm.org.uk/history/next-of-kin-memorial-plaque-scroll-and-king-s-message.

Indian Mutiny Medal Roll: search.fibis.org/frontis/bin/

Inventory of War Memorials: ukniwm.org.uk

Lives of the First World War: livesofthefirstworldwar.org

The expanding centenary crowdsourcing project ultimately aims to record as many individuals who contributed to the war effort as possible – both overseas and on the home front. Joining, browsing and uploading life stories can all be done for free, but subscribers can access various 'premium record sets' (available on Findmypast) and create online communities.

The Long, Long Trail: longlongtrail.co.uk

'A site all about the soldiers, units, regiments and battles of the British Army of the First World War, and how to research and understand them.' Its creator, Chris Baker, has a gift for explaining complicated things clearly and simply, and his brainchild is neatly designed in a way that enhances the prose. Also, he really knows his stuff. It's simply the best place to get to grips with researching a soldier who fought in the First World War. Despite the wealth of useful information here, it never leaves you feeling overwhelmed. If you want to know how regiments, divisions, corps and units functioned, and if you want to know what life was like for soldiers and how to find out more about them, this is the place to go.

Military Archives: militaryarchives.ie

Records of Ireland's Department of Defence, the Defence Forces and the Army Pensions Board.

Ministry of Defence: www.gov.uk/requests-for-personal-data-and-service-records

Holds records relating to soldiers who served after 1920 (other ranks) and 1922 (officers).

Napoleon Series: napoleon-series.org

Includes the Peninsular Roll Call – an index of officers who served with Wellington's army. It was originally compiled by Captain Lionel Challis, who began working on the project soon after the First World War. Vast parent website the Napoleon Series was launched in 1995 and boasts articles, images, maps, reviews and lots more.

National Army Museum: national-army-museum.ac.uk

The place to explore army history from 1485 to date. The site has greatly improved in recent years, and you can view sample documents, photographs and prints via the Online Collection.

National Maritime Museum: collections.rmg.co.uk

The Museum's Collections page, where you can read about and search the Archive/Library catalogue. The site also has lots of permanent and temporary exhibitions – recent examples include the Forgotten Fighters gallery which focuses on lesser known stories of the First World War.

Naval History: naval-history.net

Vast site produced and maintained by a team of specialist contributors, with sections on Royal Navy operations, honours/awards, battles, despatches and more. These include 350,000 pages of transcribed log books from the First World War.

Navy Lists: archive.org/details/nlsnavylists

Useful free resource available via archive.org are the official Navy Lists – these particular volumes scanned from the National Library of Scotland, the earliest dating from 1819 and many dating from the Second World War. You can either explore volumes through your browser or download in various formats. Information included varies but will often feature officers' dates of seniority, prizes, naval medals and ships/battles.

Operation War Diary: operationwardiary.org

Crowdsourcing project seeking to unlock the hidden stories contained within 1,500,000 million pages of First World War unit war diaries.

Peninsular War: peninsularwar.org

Prisoners of the First World War: grandeguerre.icrc.org

Search International Committee of the Red Cross lists of First World War POWs from both sides of the conflict.

RAF Museum StoryVault: rafmuseumstoryvault.org.uk

RAF's StoryVault captures stories of ordinary service men and women and also has digitised archives of conflict casualty cards, the 1918 muster roll and 1918 Air Force List. You can find out more about the RAF Museums at Cosford and London via rafmuseum.org.uk. The collections page has photographs, information about medals and uniforms, and you can buy facsimile reprints of various historic documents.

Red Cross Voluntary Aid Detachments: redcross.org.uk/ww1

The British Red Cross's Voluntary Aid Detachment records.

Register of the Anglo-Boer War 1899–1902: casus-belli.co.uk

Hosts the Anglo-Boer War Memorials Project, recording memorials across the world and currently with over 200,000 names.

Royal Army Medical Corps, Wellcome Library: wellcomelibrary.org/collections/digital-collections/royal-army-medical-corps/

Digitised archive covering more than 150 years of military medicine and wartime experiences of the Royal Army Medical Corps. It includes more than 130,000 digitised pages of correspondence, reports, personal field diaries, memoirs, photographs and memorabilia from the Army Medical Services Museum.

Royal Flying Corps 1914-18: airwar1.org.uk

Royal Leicestershire Regiment: royalleicestershireregiment.org.uk

Wonderful example of a digitised regimental archive, where you can search through over 65,000 digitised soldier records dating back to 1688, by name, army number, rank or keyword.

Each contains details from the soldier's military career including unit, period of service and where they served, and more. Photographs and links to associated medals, awards and citations are also displayed. In addition, the archive contains the full digitised Green Tiger regimental journals collection, which has documented all news and events relating to the regiment since 1904.

The Sandhurst Collection: archive.sandhurstcollection.co.uk

The Royal Military Academy's archives go back to the eighteenth century, and here you can search cadet/staff registers, containing details of almost every officer cadet that attended the Royal Military Academy Woolwich and Royal Military College Sandhurst, recording name, age, date of entry, commissioning date and corps or regiment joined. Searches are free, downloading an image costs £2.99.

Trafalgar Ancestors: apps.nationalarchives.gov.uk/trafalgarancestors/

Alongside research guides to officers and ratings of the era, you can search this TNA database of more than 18,000 individuals who fought in the Battle of Trafalgar – along with service histories/biographical details.

Unit Histories: unithistories.com

Victoria Cross: victoriacross.org.uk

Victorian Wars Forum: victorianwars.com

Waterloo Medal: nmarchive.com/our-data

Hosts the Men of Waterloo database of individuals granted the Waterloo Medal. This was the first true campaign medal as it was all given to all, regardless of rank, and was won by some 39,000 veterans.

Welsh Experience of the First World War: cymru1914.org

Western Front Association: westernfrontassociation.com

World War 1 Naval Combat: worldwar1.co.uk

FURTHER READING

Brooks, Richard and Matthew Little. *Tracing Your Royal Marine Ancestors*, Pen & Sword, 2008

Fowler, Simon. *Tracing Your Naval Ancestors*, Pen & Sword, 2011

Fowler, Simon. *Tracing Your Army Ancestors*, Pen & Sword, 2013

Fowler, Simon. *Tracing Your First World War Ancestors: A Guide for Family Historians*, Pen & Sword, 2013

Spencer, William. *Medals: the Researcher's Guide*, The National Archives, 2008

Tomaselli, Phil. *Air Force Lives*, Pen & Sword, 2013

WORKING LIVES

Research someone's employment and you find out how they lived, how they were defined by society and the community around them, about their wealth, status and day-to-day existence. But you should prepare yourself for some legwork: the kind of sources you're after can be patchy and inconsistent, are often unindexed and, depending on the industry, it is perfectly possible that you will never find any specific reference to your ancestor.

High fliers – the highly trained and well paid – tend to leave behind more of a trail than a transient labourer. You may be able to trace the careers of lawyers, bankers, doctors, nurses and architects from records of further education, examinations or apprenticeships, through to the staff registers of the firms and institutions they joined. For miners, an industry popular with students of Britain's industrial history, there are whole archives, libraries and museums dedicated to its study, and yet records relating to individual miners can still be hard to find. Skipping sideways to engineering or shipbuilding perhaps and the situation is that most firms were far more likely to have kept records of what they built, rather than the men who built them.

Even if you fail to find any records relating to your ancestor's life in the factory, field, shop floor, coalface, counter or office, there are always contemporary sources that can help you find out more about what life was like for the average worker in a particular trade at a particular time.

If you have found your ancestor in the census, you will know where they lived and you should know how the enumerator recorded their profession. You're next step is to find out what documents survive. Is there material held locally? Has it been catalogued? Is there some centralised source or archive relating to the industry in which they worked? If it's a large company or institution, does it maintain its own archive? Was there any training or system of apprenticeships in the trade? Were there professional associations that your ancestor might have joined? Was there a trade union associated with the industry?

Sources can take many forms, from handwritten documents and ledgers to printed in-company magazines, to uniforms, cap badges and photographs. Sheffield Archives has records of over 100 iron and steel businesses, including material relating to production, finance, sales and marketing, employment records and photographs. You would be very lucky to find a photograph of your ancestor at work, yet any contemporary images can give you unique insights. Sheffield Archives has pictures of the city's 'buffer girls', for example, which reveal how, as they were working with acid, they wore cloth aprons, clogs and headscarfs to work.

As we're in the area, let's travel 7 miles north-east to visit Clifton Park Museum. This is home of Rotherham's Archives and Local Studies Service, where you'll find Victorian apprenticeship indentures from the Beatson Clark glassworks collection and the Entry and Leaving Service Book from the Guest and Chrimes Brassworks, 1864. Indeed, quickly Google 'Guest and Chrimes Brassworks' and the first result (at the time of writing) is the BFI Britain on Film player where you can watch actual footage of workers leaving the Brassworks in 1901 (player.bfi.org.uk

/film/watch-workers-leaving-guest-and-chrimes-brassworks-rotherham-1901-1901/).

Just a little further north and we can drop in on the Barnsley Museum and Discovery Centre. Here there's a handwritten 1839 journal detailing the lives of workers at Elsecar Colliery, giving the names of employees, how much coal they extracted and their pay. You'll also see a lithograph printed to commemorate the 351 men and boys killed by explosions at the Oaks Colliery, Barnsley on 12 and 13 December 1866.

Further north we can visit the Heritage Hub, the Scottish Borders Archive and Local History Centre. Here there's an 1858 register of constables for Roxburghshire in which you can follow the career of one Archibald Hogarth, recording, among many other things, a minor case of misconduct when he failed to report an unshaven policeman! The Museum of Scottish Lighthouses in Fraserburgh has the visitors' book from Hoy Low lighthouse in Stromness, bearing the signatures of Robert Louis Stevenson and his father Thomas Stevenson, who was working for the Northern Lighthouse Board. Essex Record Office has registers of mainly female weavers employed at Courtaulds' silk factory in Halstead (1830–84). Ceredigion Archives in Aberystwyth has a run of material chronicling the rise and fall of Pwll Roman Lead Mine in north Cardiganshire, with monthly running costs and ledgers detailing men employed on particular days of the week, sometimes showing specific jobs they were paid to carry out.

I hope this random list of occupational treasures has captured your enthusiasm for regional archives, local history libraries and museums, and shows the potential for finding enlightening material.

In-company magazines and journals often include details of promotions and appointments, workforce socials and sporting leagues, notices of births, marriages and deaths, and sometimes detailed obituaries. Sheffield Archives holds runs of the *Bombshell*, for example, which was the official employees' journal for

The Historical Directories of England & Wales website is a really useful free resource. It has digitised trade directories covering England and Wales from the 1760s to the 1910s which you can browse online or download as PDFs.

workers at Firth Brown Steelworks. The archives of confectionery manufacturers Rowntree Mackintosh held at the Borthwick Institute in York includes *Cocoa Works Magazine*, recording employees on military service during the First World War and those killed in action. And remember that some in-company magazines and trade newspapers survive at centralised archives and libraries such as the British Library.

Agricultural labourers, or ag labs, are notoriously hard to research, but it's still worth investigating what may have survived. The names of farmers, rural craftsmen and tradesmen may well appear in family and estate collections. They may appear in account books, documenting amounts paid to local workers for products and work, or in records of tenants and rent. The tenants of cottages at the Lilleshall Estate in Shropshire, for example, are recorded in a document of 1836. Here they are listed in alphabetical order, alongside information about the type of property, their occupation, size of family, the state of repair of each property and even 'habits' – some are described as 'industrious', others as 'indifferent'.

It's rare but individual farm collections do also survive. Bedfordshire and Luton Archives has the farm account book for West End Farm, Stevington, showing each labourer's name, daily occupation and weekly sum paid. Aberdeen City and Aberdeenshire Archives has seventeenth- and eighteenth-century account books from Easter Beltie Farm, in which we find details of the 'fee' – a verbal contract between farmer and casual labourer for a half-year's work. In return for his service, John Mitchell was to be given £8 6s. 8d., 2 ells of gray (a type of cloth), two pairs of shoes, one shirt and a pair of trousers. While Shropshire Archives holds an early nineteenth-century farm bailiff's account of workmen's time, listing the names and occupations (ploughmen, labourers and carters) of men each day.

Below are some important on and offline resources, some useful for general occupational research, others specific to industries and trades. If the occupation that interests you isn't here, at the very least it will hopefully encourage you to take a look at what's out there for you. In general always start by consulting TNA, the National Records of Scotland, the National Library of Wales, PRONI and the National Archives of Ireland websites to check for any relevant research guides. Also, investigate what you can find via the county/borough archive's online catalogue, or multi-archive catalogues such as TNA's Discovery or Archives Wales (www.archiveswales.org.uk).

Identifying Occupations

If you have found your ancestor in the census, you should have an occupation. But sometimes this first hurdle can cause problems if it's an archaic or unfamiliar term. There are several sites with A–Z guides to some old, forgotten occupations.

Dictionary of Old Occupations, by Jane Jewitt:
www.familyresearcher.co.uk/glossary/Dictionary-of-Old-Occupations-Index.html
England Occupations, FamilySearch wiki:
familysearch.org/learn/wiki/en/England_Occupations
Rodney Hall: rmhh.co.uk/occup/index.html
Includes occupations listed in the 1891 census.
ScotlandsPeople:
www.scotlandspeople.gov.uk/content/help/index.aspx?r=551&430

Similarly the AddressingHistory website offers access to digitised Scottish post office directories, which can be searched by name, place or profession.

Has a list of 1,500 occupations, their definitions and variants.
GenDocs, Ranks, professions, occupations and trades:
   homepage.ntlworld.com/hitch/gendocs/trades.html
Olive Tree Genealogigy:
   www.olivetreegenealogy.com/misc/occupations.shtml
Lists medieval and obsolete English terms.
Old Occupations in Scotland: scotsfamily.com/occupations.htm

Trade Directories
Trade directories can sometimes be the only potential source left
to you of an ancestor's working life. If they ran a small shop, firm
or school, or if they were working craftsmen or artisans their
details may appear here. The most established names in trade
directories were Kelly's and Pigot's, and both become ever more
detailed over time. Most commercial sites have digitised
directories in their rosters, and in addition several firms offer them
on CD-Rom or PDF downloads. You can also access free digitised
directories from several online sources.

Historical Directories of England & Wales:
   specialcollections.le.ac.uk/cdm/landingpage/collection/p16445
   coll4
A collection of digitised trade directories covering England and
   Wales from the 1760s to the 1910s. You can browse the
   directories online or download them as PDFs.
Scottish Post Office Directories: digital.nls.uk/directories/
Free searchable hub to more than 700 digitised directories from
   the National Library of Scotland.
PRONI Street Directories: streetdirectories.proni.gov.uk
Reproduces directories from Belfast and environs dating from
   1819 to 1900.
Library Ireland: libraryireland.com
Includes digitised directories.
Sheffield Directories:
   sheffieldindexers.com/DirectoriesIndex.html

Apprentices

To become an apprentice, parents/guardians negotiated with a guild's master craftsman to agree conditions and price, which would then be recorded in an indenture. There were also pauper apprenticeships, arranged specifically by parish-level Overseers of the Poor to remove the child as a financial burden on the parish. And unlike traditional trade apprenticeships, the pauper apprentice indentures were not subject to any duty.

These records normally give name, addresses and trades of the masters, and the names of the apprentices, along with the sum the master received for the apprenticeship. Francis Wainwright was apprenticed to the joiner Henry Pearson of Bilston, Wolverhampton in April 1758. His indenture, which sits within the poor relief material from Condover's parish records at Shropshire Archives, reveals that he was sent a considerable distance to learn his trade.

Many apprenticeship records survive locally in papers of guilds, businesses, charities, families, individuals and parish collections. The Statute of Apprentices was passed in 1563, and it meant no one who had not served an apprenticeship was allowed to enter a trade. But there was no centralised record of apprentices kept in England and Wales until 1710, when stamp duty was payable on indentures of apprenticeship. The resulting registers of the duty paid are housed at TNA and you can search these apprenticeships via ancestry.co.uk or browse them on digital microfilm. There are also indexes of apprentices from 1710 to 1774 on findmypast.co.uk, which also has London Apprenticeship Abstracts (1442–1850), drawn from records of London livery companies. There are 'articles of clerkship' (1756–1874) available via Ancestry – contracts between an apprentice clerk and the attorney or solicitor – and TheGenealogist.co.uk also has a large collection of apprenticeship records.

Workhouses.org:
  workhouses.org.uk/education/apprenticeship.shtml
Part of the Children & Education section of the wonderful
  Workhouse website, detailing the workings of the
  apprenticeship system.
Apprentices and masters guide:
  nationalarchives.gov.uk/records/looking-for-
  person/apprentice.htm
People in business and trades:
  nationalarchives.gov.uk/records/looking-for-person/other-
  occupations.htm

Trade Unions

Trade Union Ancestors: www.unionancestors.co.uk
Estimates that around 5,000 trade unions have existed at one time
  or another, and that tens of millions of people have been
  members. It has an A–Z of trade unions, information about
  membership, a trade-union timeline, a list of major strikes and
  histories of many individual unions. The site's creator also runs
  the wonderful Chartist Ancestors website.
Modern Records Centre, University of Warwick:
  www2.warwick.ac.uk/services/library/mrc/
Many records relating to trade unions reside here. The website
  also has useful information about which union an ancestor
  from a particular trade or industry is likely to have joined. The
  site also has a list of commonly searched trades/occupations,
  adapted from a 1927 dictionary produced by the Ministry of
  Labour.
Trade Union Membership Registers:
  search.findmypast.co.uk/search-world-records/britain-trade-
  union-membership-registers
Findmypast has over 3 million British trade-union records from
  the Modern Records Centre, including digitised images of the
  original record books from 26 unions.

The Union Makes Us Strong, TUC History Online:
  unionhistory.info
People's History Museum: phm.org.uk/archive-study-centre/
Working Class Movement Library: www.wcml.org.uk

Agricultural Labourers, Smiths, Millers and Rural Craftsmen

The amount of surviving documentary evidence of cottage industries and rural crafts varies from place to place and industry to industry. But some very useful websites include the following.

ConnectedHistories: connectedhistories.org
This vast search hub gives access to the likes of the Victoria
  County Histories, providing local histories of parishes and
  townships, sometimes detailing the fortunes and practices of
  individual farms.
The Mills Archive: millsarchive.org
Blacksmiths Index: blacksmiths.mygenwebs.com/
This is a 'Genealogical Index of Blacksmiths', drawn mainly
  from UK census data, recording blacksmiths, wheelwrights,
  farriers and more.
Museum of English Rural Life: reading.ac.uk/merl/
Rural Museums Network: ruralmuseums.ssndevelopment.org
Irish Agricultural Museum: www.irishagrimuseum.ie
National Wool Museum: www.museumwales.ac.uk/wool/

Mining

The vast majority of mining records reside at local/county archives. After nationalisation in 1947 you need to look for records from the National Coal Board. There are summary descriptions of the archives available via Discovery (discovery.national archives.gov.uk/details/c/F182763).

Scottish Mining: scottishmining.co.uk
Database of more than 22,000 names of those involved in coal,
iron and shale mining.
Durham Mining Museum: dmm.org.uk
Mining histories, colliery maps, a Who's Who, lists of engineers
and all kinds of transcribed documents.
Coal Mining History Resource Centre: cmhrc.co.uk
Has the National Database of Mining Deaths dating back to the
1600s.
Welsh Coal Mines: welshcoalmines.co.uk
Database of mines with histories and images.
National Coal Mining Museum: ncm.org.uk
Includes details of the Museum's reference library.
Scottish Mining Museum: scottishminingmuseum.com
Tyne & Wear Archives Centre: twmuseums.org.uk/tyne-and-
wear-archives/catalogue-amp-user-guides/user-guides.html

Policing
Essex Police Museum: essex.police.uk/museum/
Has indexes to officers in the Essex County Constabulary from
the 1880s to the present day.
British Transport Police History Group: btphg.org.uk
Lists recipients of various honours, decorations and medals.
Staffordshire Name Indexes: www.staffsnameindexes.org.uk
Includes an index to Staffordshire Police Force Registers (1840–
1920) and a police disciplinary index (1857–86).
Metropolitan Police Heritage Centre: metpolicehistory.co.uk
Research collections include a 54,000-name database from 1829,
Central Records of Service from 1911 and pension cards.

Rail
Ancestry: ancestry.co.uk/cs/uk/occupations-alta
Ancestry has the Railway Employment Records (1833–1956)
collection produced in association with TNA, mainly drawn from

staff registers. It also has some railway company magazines.

Cheshire, Railway Staff Database: archives.cheshire.gov.uk/default.aspx?page=70

A database from Cheshire Archives, drawn from seventeen staff registers from four railway companies.

National Railway Museum: nrm.org.uk

Details of the NRM's library and archive. There's an online catalogue and family history advice page.

Railways Archive: railwaysarchive.co.uk

Maritime

The Registrar General of Shipping and Seamen was responsible for keeping records of merchant seamen and so most material is held in the Board of Trade record series (BT) at TNA. Important maritime collections survive in disparate archives and museums, covering fishermen, whalers, trawlermen and harbour masters.

Crew List Index Project: crewlist.org.uk

Huge database of crew lists held in various archives confined to merchant seafarers on British registered ships (1861–1913).

Maritime History Archive: www.mun.ca/mha/

Canadian archive that has lots of material relating to British merchant shipping, including Crew Lists and Agreements (1861–1913).

Welsh Mariners: welshmariners.org.uk

Includes an index of 23,500 Welsh merchant masters, mates and engineers active from 1800 to 1945.

HM Waterguard: hm-waterguard.org.uk

Dedicated to the history, men and work of the Preventive Service of HM Customs & Excise.

Register of Merchant Seamen, Southampton Archives: southampton.gov.uk/libraries-museums/local-family-history/southampton-archives/index-merchant-seamen.aspx

Information about the Central Index Register of Merchant Seamen.

Grimsby Fishermen, North East Lincolnshire Archives:
  www.nelincs.gov.uk/faqs/archives-kept-north-east-
  lincolnshire-archives/
Searchable catalogue of 38,000 Grimsby crew lists. Also looks
  after registers of fishing apprentices.
Hull History Centre: hullhistorycentre.org.uk
Has records of shipping companies, fishing crew lists (1884–
  1914) and the Sailors' Children's Society.
Irish Mariners: irishmariners.ie
Details of over 23,000 Irish-born merchant seamen.
National Maritime Museum: rmg.co.uk/national-maritime-
  museum
Lloyd's Marine Collection, Guildhall Library:
  guildhalllibrarynewsletter.wordpress.com/tag/lloyds-marine-
  collection/
East India Company, FIBIS Wiki:
  wiki.fibis.org/index.php/East_India_Company
East India Company Ships: eicships.info/index.html
Trinity House Maritime Museum: trinityhouseleith.org.uk
Coastguards of Yesteryear: coastguardsofyesteryear.org

Textiles
Spinning the Web: spinningtheweb.org.uk
Cotton Town: cottontown.org
Scottish Textile Heritage Online: scottishtextileheritage.org.uk
Derwent Valley Mills: www.derwentvalleymills.org
The Weaver's Triangle: www.weaverstriangle.co.uk

Medicine
The Wellcome Library: wellcomelibrary.org/collections/digital-
  collections/mental-healthcare/
Involved with several mass-digitisation projects including this
  Mental Healthcare project, drawing on material from the
  Library's own archives as well as partner organisations such

as Ticehurst House Hospital and the Retreat in York. Other Wellcome Library material scheduled for digitisation includes the Medical Students' Register (1882–1910) and the Dentists' Register (1879–1942).

Hospital Records Database:
nationalarchives.gov.uk/hospitalrecords

Provides information about the location of the records of UK hospitals – currently over 2,800 entries.

Wellcome Trust: wellcome.ac.uk

Provides advice aimed at those researching doctors, physicians, surgeons, apothecaries, nurses, midwives and dentists.

Royal Army Medical Corps:
wellcomelibrary.org/collections/digital-collections/royal-army-medical-corps/

British Army nurses' service records:
nationalarchives.gov.uk/records/army-nurses-service-records.htm

Search/download First World War British Army nurses' service records.

Royal College of Physicians, Munks Roll:
munksroll.rcplondon.ac.uk

British Optical Association Museum: college-optometrists.org/en/college/museyeum/

Medical Museums: medicalmuseums.org

Lothian Health Services Archives: lhsa.lib.ed.ac.uk

Engineering and Manufacturing

Ancestry: ancestry.co.uk/cs/uk/occupations-alta

Has Electrical Engineers (1871–1930) plus Civil and Mechanical Engineer Records (1820–1930).

I Worked at Raleigh: iworkedatraleigh.com

Home to video clips, stories, photographs and more relating to working life at the bicycle factory in Nottingham.

Tyne & Wear Archives: twmuseums.org.uk

Has an internationally recognised shipbuilding collection.
Institution of Civil Engineers:
  ice.org.uk/topics/historicalengineering/Archives
Institution of Mechanical Engineers:
  imeche.org/knowledge/library/archive

Banking
Bank of England History:
  bankofengland.co.uk/about/pages/history/default.aspx
Includes digitised sources and a memorial to staff killed in both
  world wars.
RBS Heritage Hub: heritagearchives.rbs.com/use-our-
  archives/your-research/british-banking-history.html
Contains information about all British and Irish banks that
  became part of RBS.
Lloyds Archives: lloydsbankinggroup.com/our-group/our-
  heritage/our-archives/
Details of staff records (registers, salary records) and a complete
  collections index.
HSBC Archives: hsbc.com/about-hsbc/company-history/hsbc-
  archives
Coutts History: coutts.com/about-us/history/

Lawyers
Lincoln's Inn Archives:
  lincolnsinn.org.uk/index.php/library/the-inns-archives
Archive of the Honourable Society of Lincoln's Inn – one of
  four Inns of Court in London to which barristers of England
  and Wales belong and where they are called to the Bar.
Gray's Inn Archives: graysinn.org.uk/history/archives
Site provides links to external digitised transcriptions of both
  the Pension Books and Register of Admissions.
Law Society Corporate Archive: lawsociety.org.uk/support-
  services/library-services/corporate-archive/

Middle Temple Archives: middletemple.org.uk/about-
   us/history/
Online sources include Register of Admissions.
Inner Temple Admissions Database:
   innertemple.org.uk/history/the-archives
Details of the Inner Temple archives including the free
   Admissions Database (1547–1920).
Law Society's Solicitors Regulation Authority: sra.org.uk
Maintains a register listing lawyers admitted since 1845.

Clergymen

Clergy of the Church of England Database:
   theclergydatabase.org.uk
Brings together biographical data of clergymen between 1540
   and 1835.
The Cause Papers Database: hrionline.ac.uk/causepapers/
Searchable catalogue of more than 14,000 cause papers relating
   to cases heard between 1300 and 1858 in the Church courts of
   the diocese of York.
Crockford's Clerical Directory: www.crockford.org.uk
Biographical details of more than 27,000 Anglican clergy.
Church of England collection, Lambeth Palace Library:
   lambethpalacelibrary.org
John Rylands Library:
   library.manchester.ac.uk/searchresources/guidetospecialcollect
   ions/methodist/using/indexofministers/
Online index of Methodist ministers.

Retail

John Lewis Memory Store: johnlewismemorystore.org.uk
Memories/photographs from the John Lewis Partnership.
Woolworths Museum: woolworthsmuseum.co.uk
The Sainsbury Archive, Museum of London:
   archive.museumoflondon.org.uk/sainsburyarchive/

Marks & Spencer Company Archive:
  marksintime.marksandspencer.com

Brewers and Publicans
Guinness Archive Index: guinness-
  storehouse.com/en/genealogysearch.aspx
Official Guinness Archive index to some 20,000 employees of
  the St James's Gate Brewery in Dublin.
Scottish Brewing Archive: archives.gla.ac.uk/sba/default.html
Has an alphabetical list of breweries and associated firms, the
  records of which are held here.
Brewery History Society: breweryhistory.com
Includes a gazetteer of pre-1940 breweries operating in England.
Pub History Society: pubhistorysociety.co.uk
Warwickshire Victuallers:
  apps.warwickshire.gov.uk/Victuallersdb/victuallers/indexes
Database of licensed victuallers between 1801 and 1828.
National Brewing Library:
  brookes.ac.uk/library/speccoll/brewing.html
Lost Pubs Project: closedpubs.co.uk
Beamish Museum: beamish.org.uk

Entertainers
The Stage Archive: archive.thestage.co.uk
Archive of the *Stage* containing previews/reviews as well as
  details of actors, theatres and performances.
Author Lloyd: arthurlloyd.co.uk
Music hall site inspired by popular performer Arthur Lloyd
  (1839–1904).
National Library of Scotland: digital.nls.uk/playbills/
Browse playbills and theatre programmes.
Scottish Theatre Archive:
  gla.ac.uk/services/specialcollections/collectionsa-
  z/scottishtheatrearchive/

National Fairground Archive: shef.ac.uk/nfa
East London Theatre Archive: elta-project.org
Theatre Collection, University of Bristol:
  bris.ac.uk/theatrecollection/
Footlight Notes: footlightnotes.tripod.com/index.html
London Music Hall Database:
  royalholloway.ac.uk/drama/Music-hall/index.asp
Royal College of Music Library & Archive:
  rcm.ac.uk/library/contactus/archivesandrecords/
British Music Hall Society: britishmusichallsociety.com
London Symphony Orchestra Archive: lso.co.uk/about-the-lso-
  archive
Scottish Music Hall & Variety Theatre Society:
  scottishmusichallsociety.webs.com

Others

The National Archives, Business/Company Records:
  nationalarchives.gov.uk/records/looking-for-
  subject/business.htm
National Records of Scotland: nrscotland.gov.uk/research/visit-
  us/scotlandspeople-centre/useful-websites-for-family-history
  -research/occupations
Occupational research guides, also linking to useful websites
  such as a Dictionary of Scottish Architects
  (www.scottisharchitects.org.uk).
Ancestry: ancestry.co.uk/cs/uk/occupations-alta
British Postal Service Appointment Books (1737–1969), Civil
  Engineer Lists (1818–1930) and Electrical Engineer Lists
  (1871–1930).
British Telecom Digital Archives: www.digitalarchives.bt.com
British Postal Museum and Archive: www.postalheritage.org.uk
Findmypast: findmypast.co.uk
Also has collections of Thames watermen and lightermen
  (1688–2010) and the Dental Surgeons Directory (1925).

Scottish Printing Archival Trust: scottishprintarchive.org
Livery Companies: liverycompanies.com
Occupations, Genuki: genuki.org.uk/big/Occupations.html
Business Archives Council of Scotland:
   www.gla.ac.uk/services/archives/bacs/
Museum of Childhood: vam.ac.uk/moc/
Working Lives Research Institute: workinglives.org
Tolpuddle Martyrs Museum: tolpuddlemartyrs.org.uk
New Lanark World Heritage Site: newlanark.org
Black County Living Museum: www.bclm.co.uk
Ulster Folk & Transport Museum: nmni.com/uftm

FURTHER READING

Emm, Adele. *Tracing Your Trade and Craftsmen Ancestors: A Guide for Family Historians*, Pen & Sword, 2015

Hawkings, David T. *Railway Ancestors*, Sutton Publishing, 2008

Tonks, David. *My Ancestor Was A Coalminer*, Society of Genealogists, 2014

Waters, Colin. *A Dictionary of Old Trades, Titles and Occupations*, Countryside Books, 2002

SECRETS, SCANDALS AND HARD TIMES

Parts of post-Industrial Revolution Britain were overcrowded, poverty-stricken and crime-ridden. While the County Asylums Act 1808 had been introduced to establish a network of institutions to care for people with mental health problems (although many counties failed), still the majority of the responsibility of care for the destitute, disabled, orphaned and abandoned fell on the shoulders of an already overstretched and piecemeal system of local poor relief. In England and Wales this pressure on the parish eventually led to a new network of Poor Law unions, each with its own workhouse.

The Poor Law and the Union Workhouse

Generally, the term 'Poor Law' can be used to describe the various systems that were in place prior to the creation of the modern welfare state. These are grouped into the Old Poor Law (dating back to the reign of Queen Elizabeth) and the New Poor Law (passed in England and Wales in 1834). In brief, before that date most care of the poor fell on the shoulders of the parish. Therefore, the primary sources for the poverty stricken are parish level, such as settlement certificates and examinations, removal orders and other records of the Overseers of the Poor.

After 1834 this haphazard system was replaced by a system of Poor Law unions, run by an elected board of guardians, which administered workhouses (although workhouses did exist in many areas prior to the creation of the new unions). Records of individual Poor Law unions normally survive at county record offices, while records of the presiding Poor Law Commission survive at TNA.

Similarly, in Ireland a Poor Law Act of 1838 divided the country into 159 Poor Law unions, each with an elected board of guardians to administer relief. So, as in England and Wales, the kind of resources you may find are board of guardian minutes and workhouse registers, which can include names, dates of admission, places of birth or residence, occupations and more. Many survive in county level and national collections.

The situation in Scotland is similar in that following the Reformation the responsibility for the poor fell on the parish, through heritors (local landowners) and the kirk sessions – the Church courts responsible for each parish. There was a parish poor fund, drawn from donations, fines and services. Heritors' records (where they survive) and kirk session minute books and accounts usually include lists of paupers and relief paid (although often recorded in among all other financial business).

New Poor Law dates from an Act of 1845 when parochial boards were set up in each parish to administer poor relief. The records of parochial boards are generally found in local authority archives. Research gets a lot easier in 1864 when standardised poor relief registers were introduced. The Scottish Poor Relief System also differed from the English one in that parishes did not have to set up their own poorhouse, they just had to be able to provide 'indoor' or 'outdoor' relief.

You can find out more via National Records of Scotland (nrscotland.gov.uk/research/guides/poor-relief-records), as well as searching the online catalogue for heritors' and kirk session records. They also hold records of Destitution Boards, set up in the 1840s to deal with widespread poverty in the Highlands following the failure of the potato crop.

London Metropolitan Archives' Boards of Guardians series of records start around 1830 and include material from workhouses, asylums and special schools. It also holds records from over 100 hospitals, including the former county lunatic asylums of Hanwell, Colney Hatch and Banstead. The East Riding of Yorkshire archives in Beverley have collections relating to the Society for the Reformation of Juvenile Offenders for the North and East Ridings (later known as Castle Howard Reformatory School), as well as records of the Yorkshire Catholic Reform School.

Poor Law material can be enlightening, riveting and shocking. Bedfordshire's surviving Poor Law collections include pauper applications which can give name and age of applicant, wife and children, settlement, description, disability and other details, including names of relatives 'capable of assisting'. The Kempston Overseers' account book includes one 1758 entry recording 1s. paid for Ann Jervice's 'Wooden Legg', alongside detailed assessments, boarding out agreements, and miscellaneous receipts for casual wages paid to paupers and sale of paupers' goods.

Poor Law records can take many forms. At Shropshire Archives there's a seventeenth-century journal with recipes and remedies kept by one Ann Whittle, which later includes what appear to be poor relief entries. It also has Ludlow Poor Law Union's 'clothing deposited book', recording the clothing that individuals had with them on entering the workhouse. There are also punishment books, documenting offences and punishments – standard punishments include meals of bread and water and picking oakum. Highland Archive Centre has the Inverness Poorhouse Admission Register, recording name, age, status, employment, religious denomination and any disability. A page from the Easter Ross Union Poorhouse Inmates Register from 1897 records a new baby named Victoria Diamond Jubilee.

OTHER RESOURCES

The Workhouse: workhouses.org.uk

An encyclopaedic guide to the workhouse system across Scotland, Wales, Ireland and England, boasting all kinds of background material about how the system developed, the kinds of records it created, as well as detailed illustrated histories of workhouses, searchable by Poor Law location. There's also a fairly comprehensive list of archives across UK and Ireland that hold Poor Law records. There's also the sister site childrenshomes. org.uk, which details of orphanages, reformatories and industrial schools.

Poor Law Unions' Gazette: britishnewspaperarchive.co.uk

One of thousands of titles digitised from the British Library's vast newspaper collections, the *Poor Law Unions' Gazette* mainly carried descriptions of men who had left their families.

Surrey Poor Law Unions: exploringsurreyspast.org.uk/indexes/

Surrey History Centre site with various online indexes including the Chertsey Poor Law Union admission and discharge books and Godstone Poor Law Union application and report books.

FamilySearch:

familysearch.org/learn/wiki/en/England_and_Wales_Poor_La w_Records_1834-1948

FamilySearch's guide to the Poor Law records of England and

Wales includes links to digital collections from Norfolk, Kent and Cheshire.

Ancestry: search.ancestry.co.uk/search/db.aspx?dbid=1557

Has vast Poor Law and Board of Guardian Records from the London Metropolitan Archives, as well as collections from Warwickshire, Dorset and Norfolk.

Findmypast: findmypast.co.uk/articles/world-records/search-all-uk-records/institution-and-organisation—records

Has London Poor Law abstracts, and material from Lincolnshire, Cheshire, Derbyshire and Manchester.

One of the most fascinating free resources available is the Old Bailey Online website – a fully searchable edition of 197,745 criminal trials held at London's central criminal court.

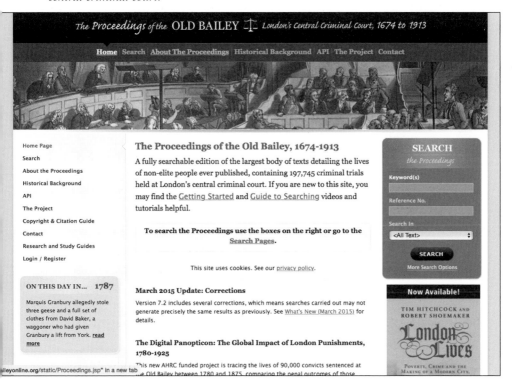

Waifs and Strays Society: hiddenlives.org.uk
Charitable society that cared for 22,500 children.
London Lives: Crime, Poverty & Social Policy in the Metropolis:
   londonlives.org
Ragged School Museum: raggedschoolmuseum.org.uk
Foundling Museum: foundlingmuseum.org.uk

Crime and Punishment

Most of us enjoy some black sheepery on our family tree. And if your ancestor was accused or convicted of a crime, there are a host of police records, court records, prison sources and more, where you may be able to find traces. In addition, of course, if the crime was at all sensational it may have been reported in local or national newspapers.

As with many research subjects, identifying where any sources are likely to survive is often a first step. Minor misdemeanours are likely to have been dealt with locally, more serious criminality at higher courts. The Ludlow Borough Collection, for example, includes the Council of the Marches of Wales, which sat at Ludlow Castle. A record dating from March 1621 documents the case of William Webbe, accused of forgery and bribery. He would have been forced to stand in the pillory in Ludlow on market day with a piece of paper, probably worn as a hat, declaring his misdemeanours. The Scottish Borders Archive and Local History Centre has an entry in the Burgh of Jedburgh Council Record, dated 1662, referring to preparations for a witch trial. 'The counsell ordainit the deacons to namine six of evrie trade to attend the commissioners appoyntit trying and judging of ye witches upon Wednisday nixt.'

Thankfully, there are a number of excellent sources of advice, with lots of sample material, as well as many expanding online databases available through free and commercial hubs. TNA, for example, has guides to convict transportation, prisoners, civil litigants and bankrupts/debtors. You should also try the Crime and

Criminals guide at the National Records of Scotland (nrscotland.gov.uk), and it's allied guide to court records.

Prison records can be enlightening where they survive. Bedfordshire and Luton Archives and Records Service has Bedfordshire Quarter Sessions Rolls 1830–1900 and county gaol records. The allied register notes offence, when tried, marks and previous convictions, often with a photograph of each prisoner. TNA has digitised its prisoner photograph albums from Wandsworth Prison from the 1870s, which included physical descriptions, date of birth, crime, sentence, place of conviction and residence after release.

One particularly amazing free resource is the Proceedings of the Old Bailey (www.oldbaileyonline.org), where you can explore transcribed details of 197,745 criminal trials held at London's central criminal court from 1674 to 1913. You can search by various fields including punishment, filtering results by imprisonment, hard labour, house of correction, Newgate or penal servitude.

When delving into court material it is important to find out in which court a trial was heard: police or magistrates' court, quarter sessions or assizes, or church courts. Generally, TNA has records of the assizes, while records of quarter sessions/petty sessions held at magistrates' courts will be at local archives. The National Library of Wales has its Crime & Punishment Database (www.llgc.org.uk/sesiwn_fawr/index_s.htm), where you can search gaol files of the Court of Great Sessions in Wales from 1730 until its abolition in 1830. The Court could try all types of crimes, from petty thefts to high treason.

Another wonderful online resource is the Cause Papers Database, drawn from the Diocese of York collection at (hrionline.ac.uk/causepapers/). This has details of cases heard between 1300 and 1858 in York's Church courts, which had jurisdiction over cases involving issues of matrimony, defamation, tithe matters, probate and more. Similarly, London Lives (londonlives.org) is a wonderful place to familiarise yourself with the potential sources for researching crime and prison life in the Metropolis (between 1690 and 1800). It has court records from the City of London, Middlesex and Westminster Sessions.

Remember too that if an ancestor died in unexplained circumstances there may have been a coroner's inquest. Up to 1752 coroners handed records to assize judges, although inquests held from 1860 were filed through the quarter sessions so will generally be at local archives. The Scottish equivalent are Fatal Accident Inquiries which were processed through sheriff courts.

Always have a look at what's been produced by local archives, family history societies and museums. At the Lancaster Castle website (lancastercastle.com/Archives), for example, there is a complete Convict Database, listing inmates who were tried and sentenced at Lancaster Assizes. While the Centre for Buckinghamshire Studies has an online database of prisoners from Aylesbury Gaol. Inveraray Jail (www.inverarayjail.co.uk/the-jails-story/prison-records.aspx) has records for over 4,000 former prisoners.

OTHER RESOURCES

Ancestry: search.ancestry.co.uk/search/db.aspx?dbid=1590
Ancestry's has digitised TNA criminal registers for England and Wales, which provide dates and locations of court hearings. Other collections include a Bedfordshire Gaol Index (1770–1882), Debtors' Prison Registers (1734–1862), Birmingham prisoners (1880–1913), Prison Hulk Registers (1802–49) and the Australian Transportation series.
Findmypast: search.findmypast.co.uk/search-world-records/crime-prisons-and-punishment
Also has a database drawn from TNA material, including the Home Office calendar of prisoners (1869–1929).
Convict Transportation Registers Database: www.slq.qld.gov.au/resources/family-history/convicts
Information on 123,000 convicts transported to Australia

between 1787 and 1867.

Blacksheep Ancestors:
  blacksheepancestors.com/uk/prisons.shtml

Plymouth Prisoners:
  plymouth.gov.uk/cemeterymortuaryworkhouse

Scottish Prison Service: sps.gov.uk/Prisons/prisons.aspx

Debtors, Victorian Crime & Punishment:
  vcp.e2bn.org/justice/page11365-debtors.html

National Records of Scotland:
  nrscotland.gov.uk/research/research-guides/court-and-legal-records

British Newspaper Archive: britishnewspaperarchive.co.uk

Newspaper reports may represent the only surviving account of some cases and inquests.

Public Record Office of Northern Ireland:
  www.proni.gov.uk/index/search_the_archives/proninames/coroners__inquest__papers_-_whats_available.htm

Bastardy

Records of bastardy usually reside at parish level – they are often grouped together with Poor Law and parish chest material – or among quarter sessions records. The records were primarily concerned with establishing (and so avoiding) responsibility for providing for a bastard child under the Poor Law. If an unmarried woman was expecting a child, parish officials pressured her to reveal the father's name so the father, not the parish, had financial responsibility for the child's care. This system produced the bastardy bond (also known as a 'bond of indemnification'), which was the father's guarantee of responsibility for the child.

Shropshire Archives holds a bastardy examination from Condover Parish Records, dated 12 January 1795. It reads: 'Ann Jones met a man whom she did not then and doth not now know dressed in a green coat and had the appearance of a gentleman, in a birch coppy between Frodesley and Chatwell in the said county, and that the said man had then and there carnal knowledge of the body of her the said Ann Jones and that the said man is the father of the child of the said Ann Jones.'

The wonderful London Lives website has a page (www.londonlives.org/static/Bastardy.jsp) focusing on Bastardy Records in the capital, including case studies drawn from surviving records. The website allows you to explore the 1787 bastardy examination dated relating to Margaret Cary, and the birth of her son Richard, held at the Westminster Archives Centre. London Lives includes two long series of examinations for the parishes of St Clement Danes and St Botolph Aldgate covering *c.* 1740–1800, and a Register of Pauper Settlement and Bastardy Examinations (RD) for St Clement Danes, 1703–7.

Divorce

Before 1858, a full divorce required a private Act of Parliament – so, as you might expect, this was only available to people with means. It was the Matrimonial Causes Act of 1857 that enabled couples to obtain a divorce through civil proceedings. It also required a husband to prove his wife's adultery if he wanted a divorce, while a wife had to prove her husband's adultery and also that he had either treated her with cruelty, deserted her or committed incest or bigamy. The Herbert Divorce Act of 1937 saw the introduction of new grounds for divorce including adultery, desertion, cruelty and incurable insanity. No petition for divorce could be made in the first three years of marriage, except under exceptional circumstances. The Legal Assistance Plan of 1949 gave legal aid to the less well-off, causing an increase in the number of divorces. The Divorce Reform Act (1969) made the irretrievable breakdown of a marriage the sole ground necessary for a divorce.

You can browse lists of private Acts of Parliament to check for divorces before 1858 (www.legislation.gov.uk/changes/chron-tables/private).

Divorce case files can contain petitions, certificates and copies of the decrees nisi and absolute. The decrees absolute give the names of the petitioner, respondent and (if applicable) co-respondent and the date and place of the marriage.

The Supreme Court and some county courts grant divorces in England and Wales. Historic records of divorce petitions can be searched at TNA. Bigamous marriages were often tried in assize courts and you can research trials in Wales held before 1830 via the National Library of Wales.

TNA's English and Welsh divorce case files (1858–1914) can be accessed through Ancestry. You can also search for divorce cases via Discovery. You can also request copies of a decree absolute in England and Wales (from 1858 to present), via gov.uk/copy-decree-absolute-final-order.

Meanwhile, in Northern Ireland divorces were (rarely) granted at the Royal Courts of Justice in Belfast or at county court.

To find out more about researching divorce in Scotland you should visit the research guide produced by the National Records of Scotland. As it describes, records of 'most divorces in Scotland are listed or indexed in some way and are relatively accessible'.

From 1560 the Court of Session, and then from 1563 the Commissary Court of Edinburgh, exercised jurisdiction in divorce and separation cases. Divorce was allowed in Scotland on the grounds of adultery from 1560 and on the grounds of desertion from 1573. Before cruelty became a ground for divorce in 1938, judicial separation was one of the main legal remedies.

According to the NRS guide:

During this period Scottish matrimonial law took on a life of its own and much of the former church or canon law died away. Nevertheless, the effort and expense it took to obtain a divorce, combined with the prevalence of various types of irregular marriage, which ranged in type from the reasonably respectable to the downright dubious, acted together as a strong brake on the numbers of people seeking a formal dissolution of their marriage through the courts.

During the twentieth century the grounds for divorce widened beyond desertion and adultery to include anti-social behaviour, cruelty and non-cohabitation.

From 1830 the Court of Session replaced Edinburgh Commissary Court as the court with exclusive jurisdiction in cases of marriage, divorce and bastardy. From around 1835 (up to 1984) individual divorce cases are listed in the NRS catalogue (nrscotland.gov.uk/research/catalogues-and-indexes).

Earlier divorces can be found in *The Commissariot of Edinburgh – Consistorial Processes and Decreets, 1658–1800* (Scottish Record Society, 1909). You can read it online via scottishrecord society.org.uk. Follow the links to Old Series, then scroll down to volume thirty-four, and 'read online' leads to a digitised copy on archive.org. Remember that in Scotland a married woman traditionally retained her maiden name, so in the indexes and records she may be designated as 'Mary Smith, wife of . . . '.

Adoption

While there are official adoption records, some of which are available online, many adoptions were informal and so confirming details may prove difficult or impossible. That said, every family historian should keep in mind the history and mechanics of the adoption system, as it can often explain an anomaly in your family tree. A number of social and economic factors may lie behind cases of adoption – the death of a parent (or parents), divorce, an illegitimate birth, desertion or abandonment. Often poverty-stricken parents would seek out adoptive parents in the hope that this would give their child a chance for a better life.

First and foremost, it's important to know the legal process at the time period you're researching. And a key event was the

Adoption of Children Act of 1926. Prior to this adoptions were usually informal affairs conducted between the child's parents or guardians and the adoptive parents. Often a child would simply be taken in by other family members, friends or neighbours. Some adoptees would retain their original name, while others might take the family name of the adoptive parents. From 1927 all adoptions had to be approved by magistrates meeting in a Petty Sessions Court and each court maintained a register, which remained closed to public inspection for seventy-five years.

Similarly, in Scotland, before the Adoption of Children (Scotland) Act (1930), adoptions were arranged on a private basis. Since then adoption has been arranged by charitable bodies, local authority social work departments and then ratified by civil courts – mainly local sheriff courts. And the Registrar General for Scotland has maintained the Adopted Children Register since 1930.

Adoptions were also arranged by societies such as the Church of England Children's Society, which kept records of the adoptions it arranged. Also, there's a chance of references to adoption cases surviving in Boards of Guardians and parish chest material.

To find out more try www.gov.uk/adoption-records to nrscotland.gov.uk/research/guides/adoption-records.

FURTHER READING

Higginbotham, Peter. *A Grim Almanac of the Workhouse*, The History Press, 2013

Higginbotham, Peter. *The Workhouse Encyclopedia*, The History Press, repr. 2014

Probert, Rebecca. *Divorced, Bigamist, Bereaved?*, Takeaway Publishing, 2015

Peter Higginbotham's workhouses.org.uk

Chapter 5

FURTHER RESOURCES

WEBSITES
Useful
1911 Census: 1911census.co.uk
British Genealogy Network: britishgenealogy.net
British History Online: www.british-history.ac.uk
Connected Histories: connectedhistories.org
Cyndi's List: cyndislist.com
FamilySearch: familysearch.org
FreeBMD: freebmd.org.uk
Free UK Genealogy: freeukgenealogy.org.uk
Genuki: genuki.org.uk
Rootsweb: rootsweb.ancestry.com
ScotlandsPeople: scotlandspeople.gov.uk
UK BMD: ukbmd.org.uk
UK GDL: ukgdl.org.uk

National
British Library: bl.uk
Federation of Family History Societies: ffhs.org.uk
The National Archives: nationalarchives.gov.uk
The National Archives of Ireland: nationalarchives.ie
The National Library of Ireland: nli.ie
The National Library of Scotland: nls.uk
The National Library of Wales: llgc.org.uk
The National Records of Scotland: nrscotland.gov.uk

Public Record Office of Northern Ireland: proni.gov.uk
Scottish Association of FHSs: safhs.org.uk
Society of Genealogists: sog.org.uk
Wellcome Library: wellcomelibrary.org

Finding Aids
AIM25: aim25.ac.uk
Archives Hub: archiveshub.ac.uk
Archives Wales: archiveswales.org.uk
Discovery, The National Archives:
   discovery.nationalarchives.gov.uk
Scottish Archive Network: scan.org.uk

Subscription/Pay-per-view
Ancestry: ancestry.co.uk
AncestryDNA: dna.ancestry.co.uk
British Newspaper Archive: britishnewspaperarchive.co.uk
BMDregisters: BMDregisters.co.uk
DeceasedOnline: deceasedonline.com
FamilyRelatives: familyrelatives.com
Findmypast: findmypast.co.uk
Forces War Records: forces-war-records.co.uk
TheGenealogist: thegenealogist.co.uk
GenesReunited: genesreunited.co.uk
MyHeritage: myheritage.com

England
Cause Papers Database, Diocese of York:
   hrionline.ac.uk/causepapers/
City of Westminster Archives Centre:
   www.westminster.gov.uk/archives
Electoral Registers: electoralregisters.org.uk
Guildhall Library: cityoflondon.gov.uk
Hearth Tax Online: hearthtax.org.uk

Historical Directories:
  specialcollections.le.ac.uk/cdm/landingpage/collection/p16445
  coll4
Lancashire Lantern: lanternimages.lancashire.gov.uk
Lincs To The Past: www.lincstothepast.com
London Lives: londonlives.org
London Metropolitan Archives: cityoflondon.gov.uk
North East Inheritance Database:
  familyrecords.dur.ac.uk/nei/data/intro.php
Sheffield Indexers: sheffieldindexers.com
Staffordshire Name Indexes: www.staffsnameindexes.org.uk
Warwickshire's Past Unlocked:
  archivesunlocked.warwickshire.gov.uk/calmview/
West Yorkshire Tithe Maps Project: tracksintime.wyjs.org.uk
Windows on Warwickshire:
  www.windowsonwarwickshire.org.uk

Ireland
Association of Professional Genealogists in Ireland: apgi.ie
Catholic parish registers: registers.nli.ie
Census of Ireland 1901/1911: census.nationalarchives.ie
Documenting Ireland: Parliament, People & Migration:
  dippam.ac.uk
Dublin City Archives: www.dublincity.ie
Genealogical Society of Ireland: familyhistory.ie
Griffith's Valuation: askaboutireland.ie
Ireland: ireland.ie
Irish Ancestors: irishancestors.ie
Irish Ancestral Research Association: tiara.ie
Irish Family History Foundation: irish-roots.ie
Irish Family History Society: ifhs.ie
Irish Genealogical Research Society: igrsoc.org
Irish Genealogy: irishgenealogy.ie
Irish Times: irishtimes.com/ancestor

RootsIreland: rootsireland.ie
Tithe Applotment Books:
 titheapplotmentbooks.nationalarchives.ie/search/tab/home.jsp

Northern Ireland
Armagh Ancestry: www.armagh.co.uk/place/armagh-ancestry/
Belfast, the Linen Hall: linenhall.com
Belfast Street Directories: lennonwylie.co.uk
Derry Genealogy Centre: derry.brsgenealogy.com
General Register Office Northern Ireland:
 nidirect.gov.uk/family-history
Irish World: www.irish-world.com
Street Directories, Public Record Office of Northern Ireland:
 streetdirectories.proni.gov.uk
Ulster Historical Foundation: www.ancestryireland.com

Scotland
Aberdeen City and Aberdeenshire Archives:
 aberdeencity.gov.uk/archives
Addressing History: addressinghistory.edina.ac.uk
Am Baile, Highland History & Culture: ambaile.org.uk
Edinburgh City Archives:
 www.edinburgh.gov.uk/info/20032/access_to_information/600
 /edinburgh_city_archives
Glasgow Family History, Mitchell Library:
 glasgowfamilyhistory.org.uk
Glasgow & West of Scotland FHS: gwsfhs.org.uk
Highland FHS: highlandfamilyhistorysociety.org
John Gray Centre – Library, Museum & Archive:
 johngraycentre.org
Lothian Lives: lothianlives.org.uk.
Lothians FHS: lothiansfhs.org
National Register of Archives for Scotland:
 www.nas.gov.uk/nras/

Scotland BDM Exchange: sctbdm.com
ScotlandsPeople Centre: scotlandspeoplehub.gov.uk
ScotlandsPlaces: scotlandsplaces.gov.uk
Scotsman Archive: archive.scotsman.com
Scottish Catholic Archives: scottishcatholicarchives.org.uk
Scottish Indexes: scottishindexes.com
Scottish Post Office Directories: digital.nls.uk/directories/
Scottish Screen Archive: ssa.nls.uk

Wales
Cymru 1914: cymru1914.org
Cynefin: cynefin.archiveswales.org.uk
Digging up the Past: diggingupthepast.org.uk
National Library of Wales, Crime & Punishment Database:
  www.llgc.org.uk/sesiwn_fawr/index_s.htm
North Wales BMD: northwalesbmd.org.uk
Welsh Coal Mines: welshcoalmines.co.uk
Welsh Mariners: welshmariners.org.uk
Welsh Newspapers Online: newspapers.library.wales

General
Archive.org: archive.org
Archives New Zealand: archives.govt.nz
Britain on Film: player.bfi.org.uk/britain-on-film/
Building History: buildinghistory.org
Chartist Ancestors: chartists.net
Ellis Island: ellisisland.org
Gazettes Online: www.thegazette.co.uk
GENFair: GENFair.co.uk
HistoryPin: historypin.org
Immigrant Ships Transcribers Guild: immigrantships.net
Isle of Man Museum: imuseum.im
Library & Archives Canada: bac-lac.gc.ca/eng
Mayflower 400: mayflower400uk.co.uk

National Archives, America: archives.gov
National Archives of Australia: naa.gov.au
Parish Chest: parishchest.com
Probate Search, GOV.uk: probatesearch.service.gov.uk/#wills
Proceedings of the Old Bailey: www.oldbaileyonline.org
Ships List: theshipslist.com
US Immigrant Ancestors Project: immigrants.byu.edu
Waifs and Strays Society: hiddenlives.org.uk
The Workhouse: workhouses.org.uk

Military
Age of Nelson: ageofnelson.org
Anglo-Afghan War: garenewing.co.uk/angloafghanwar/
Anglo Boer War: angloboerwar.com
Battle of Britain Memorial: battleofbritainmemorial.org
British Medals Forum: britishmedalforum.com
Commonwealth War Graves Commission: cwgc.org
Cross & Cockade International: www.crossandcockade.com
Fleet Air Arm Archive: fleetairarmarchive.net
Great War Staffordshire: staffordshiregreatwar.com
Imperial War Museums: iwm.org.uk
Lives of the First World War: livesofthefirstworldwar.org
The Long, Long Trail: www.longlongtrail.co.uk
Medals of the World: medals.org.uk
National Army Museum: national-army-museum.ac.uk
Naval History: naval-history.net
Operation War Diary: operationwardiary.org
RAF Museum StoryVault: rafmuseumstoryvault.org.uk
Royal Flying Corps 1914–18: airwar1.org.uk
Sandhurst Collection: archive.sandhurstcollection.co.uk
Trafalgar Ancestors:
   www.nationalarchives.gov.uk/trafalgarancestors/
UK MFH: ukmfh.org.uk
Unit Histories: unithistories.com

Victorian Wars Forum: victorianwars.com

Overseas/Special Interest Groups
Anglo German FHS: agfhs.org
Anglo-Italian FHS: anglo-italianfhs.org.uk
Association of Genealogists and Researchers in Archives: agra.org.uk
Australasian Federation of Family History Organisations: affho.org
British Association for Local History: balh.co.uk
Catholic FHS: catholic-history.org.uk/cfhs
Families In British India Society: fibis.org
Federation of Family History Societies: ffhs.org.uk
Federation of Genealogical Societies, USA: fgs.org
Guild of One-Name Studies: one-name.org
Heraldry Society: theheraldrysociety.com
Huguenot Society of Great Britain and Ireland: huguenotsociety.org.uk
Institute of Heraldic & Genealogical Studies: ihgs.ac.uk
Jewish Genealogical Society of Great Britain: jgsgb.org.uk
New Zealand Society of Genealogists: genealogy.org.nz
Quaker FHS: qfhs.co.uk
Romany and Traveller FHS: rtfhs.org.uk
Society of Australian Genealogists: sag.org.au

MISCELLANEOUS
In this book I have attempted to cover lots of different subjects and sources. In this final section, I'm going to do a little mopping up, tackling some useful sources that haven't yet been covered in detail.

Coroners' Inquests
If your ancestor died in unexplained circumstances there may have been a coroner's inquest, often conducted at a local

alehouse, workhouse or building where the death occurred. Up to 1752 coroners handed records to assize judges (which were eventually transferred to TNA). But inquests held from 1860 were filed through the quarter sessions – meaning those that survive will usually be at local archives.

PRONI looks after coroners' records from 1872 to 1997, and 6,206 files/papers relating to inquests are now referenced via the online Name Search (www.proni.gov.uk/index/search_the_ archives /proninames/coroners_inquest_papers_-_whats_available. htm). The database entries contain name, address, date of death and date of inquest of the deceased. The actual papers themselves record much more information such as the name of the coroner, circumstances of death and names of jurors. London Lives has a page on Coroners' Inquests into Suspicious Deaths (londonlives. org/static/IC.jsp), where you can freely explore digital images and transcriptions from around 5,000 inquests from the City of London, Middlesex and Westminster. In Scotland the equivalent to coroners' inquests are the Fatal Accident Inquiries, which were processed through the sheriff courts. There's a useful guide available via the National Records of Scotland (nrscotland. gov.uk/research/guides/fatal-accident-inquiry-records).

Other websites include Salisbury Inquests (salisbury inquests.wordpress.com), Hertfordshire Coroners' Inquests (hertsdirect.org/services/leisculture/heritage1/hals/famhist/corone r/) and the Sussex Record Society site, which gives free access to Notes of Post Mortem Inquisitions Taken In Sussex 1485 and 1649 (sussexrecordsociety.org). Finally, there's TNA's guide at: nationalarchives.gov.uk/records/looking-for-person/coroners-inquests.htm.

Debtors and Bankrupts

The first thing to understand is the difference between 'debtors' and 'bankrupts'. Bankrupts were traders who were legally declared insolvent because of inability to pay debts. In practice many bankrupts were not traders, and bankruptcy was later extended to include craftsmen. Meanwhile, debtors, or more correctly 'insolvent debtors', were individuals unable to pay their debts – and they could not apply for bankruptcy until after 1861.

You can search the Gazette website (www.thegazette.co.uk), the official public record, for the printed notices of bankrupts. These were published by officials to inform creditors about their proceedings.

Ancestry has a collection of Debtors' Prison Registers (search.ancestry.co.uk/search/group/uk_debtors_prison) digitised from documents held at TNA. These detail over 700,000 criminals detained in Marshalsea, King's Bench and Fleet Prisons between 1734 and 1862. You can also read about debtors via Victorian Crime & Punishment (vcp.e2bn.org/justice/page11365-debtors.html).

Deeds

Deeds are often overlooked by family historians. They record the transfer of property and have the potential to add much colour to your family history research. The information contained in the documents varies a great deal, but can reveal the conditions in which your ancestor lived, and of course are especially enlightening if the building in question no longer exists. Most deeds should include a fairly detailed description of the type and location of the property, sometimes with an accompanying plan. It should also tell you who owns and/or lives in the property, but may also list previous owners and tenants, sometimes going back many years. The occupations of individuals are often recorded, sometimes with former places of residence. If property has been passed down, deeds can give information about many generations of the same family. Finally, if the land was left in a will, then the deed should record the date of death, will and probate.

Part of the problem is that collections of deeds are often

unindexed. The collection of deeds at Tower Hamlets Local History Library and Archives in London is very popular with researchers precisely because it has been indexed in great detail, by name and place. Every single individual mentioned in the records has been indexed, whether owner or tenant – that's upwards of 25,000 names.

Another example comes from West Yorkshire, where the Archive Service's Wakefield Headquarters looks after the West Riding Registry of Deeds (www.archives.wyjs.org.uk/archives-wrrd.asp). So, if your ancestors owned or leased land in the West Riding, it is possible that they will appear in the Deeds Registry, which holds indexes to 14 million deeds registered between 1704 and 1970. The registered copies are summaries of the full original deed and will tell you the names of all the parties and the location of the land involved.

Interestingly, from 1766 to 1794 there are a series of notes and drawings written in among the registry entries, revealing topical themes and evidence of personal antagonisms between the staff. Timothy Topham, Deputy Registrar from 1766 and 1810 was the victim of derogatory remarks and drawings, and was regularly referred to as 'Old Gropham'.

Electoral Rolls and Poll Books
Election records, specifically the rolls of those eligible and registered to vote, are very useful for genealogists. The 1848 Poll Book of the Borough of Leeds, for example, contains almost 28,000 surnames recorded from 31 polling districts in November 1868. This was the first election held in the UK in which more than a million votes were cast – nearly triple the number of the previous election. The result saw William Gladstone's Liberals increase their majority over Benjamin Disraeli's Conservatives. Not only are the names of the inhabitants (including some lodgers and many people never to be found in trade directories) listed here, but also the candidates they voted for.

Election records become more useful and complete as more people became eligible to vote. The timeline runs as follows:

1832   Only men with property could vote.
1867   Men with property worth £5 per annum, or tenants paying £12 per annum.
1884   Male householders/tenants paying £10 per annum could vote.
1918   Men over 21 and married women over 30 could vote.
1928   All women over 21 could vote.
1969   Men and women over 18 could vote.

Only a very small percentage of the population could vote before 1832, and poll books from this period should give details of name and parish, and details of the estate that qualified the person to vote.

Many archives and local history libraries have collections of election material off and online. Via the Essex Record Office website you can browse the county's electoral registers. Ancestry has London Electoral Registers covering the period 1835 to 1965, while Findmypast is working with the British Library to index Electoral Registers.

The National Records of Scotland has this useful guide to directories and electoral records www.gro-scotland.gov.uk/research/visit-us/scotlandspeople-centre/useful-websites-for-family-history-research/directories-registers-electoral-rolls. Remember too that some Scottish archives hold Burgess Rolls – burgesses were inhabitants who held land and contributed to the town and only burgesses could enjoy certain privileges, including the right to vote.

PRONI has digitised its Freeholders' records (www.proni.gov.uk/index/search_the_archives/freeholders_records.htm). These were lists of freeholders who were entitled to vote, arranged on a county basis and comprise the registers (those who had registered to vote) and poll books (lists of voters and the candidates for whom they voted). It has digitised around 5,500 sheets from pre-1840 registers and poll books, which have also been indexed. You can search here: apps.proni.gov.uk/ freeholders/Default.aspx.

Estate Collections and Family Papers

We touched on estate records in Chapter 4, Working Lives as they can sometimes help in researching rural craftsmen and agricultural labourers who lived or worked on the estate. More and more family collections have been catalogued, but detailed indexes and finding aids are still relatively rare. One important thing to remember about estate and family collections is that documents relating to one area may often be found in other archives. If a noble family from one area owned land or estates in another county, documents relating to these estates may well remain with the 'parent' archive in the county where they lived.

The National Archives guide to Estate & Manorial records is at nationalarchives.gov.uk/records/looking-for-place/landed estates.htm, and you can search for estate papers via Discovery, which also includes the Manorial Documents Register of England and Wales. These Manorial Documents are defined as court rolls, surveys, maps, terriers, documents and books relating to the boundaries, franchises, wastes, customs or courts of a manor. The equivalent National Records of Scotland guide (nrscotland. gov.uk/research/guides/estate-records) covers types of records such as rent rolls, leases (tacks) and household accounts.

There are lots of other websites that can give you a picture of the kind of material estate collections may include. The Staffordshire and Stoke-on-Trent Archive Service created the Sutherland Collection website (www.sutherlandcollection. org.uk), a fully indexed website built around the Leveson-Gower family archive, Marquesses of Stafford and Dukes of Sutherland, which contains many thousands of names – employees, tenants, shopkeepers and suppliers, savers in the Trentham Savings Bank and workers on the building of Trentham Hall. There's also the Lives and Livelihoods in Conisbrough Manor. (hrionline.ac.uk/conisbrough/) and the Arley Hall Archives 1750–90 (arleyhall archives.co.uk).

Medieval Sources and Research

Medieval records can be hard to access and difficult to interpret. MedievalGenealogy (medievalgenealogy.org.uk) is a good place to start. It explores potential medieval sources such as manorial records, government enrolments, taxation returns, heraldic visitations and court material. There's also the Foundation for Medieval Genealogy: fmg.ac.

There are several name-rich databases online. England's Immigrants Database (englandsimmigrants.com) contains 64,000 names of people known to have migrated to England between 1330 and 1550. While the Henry III Fine Rolls Project (frh3.org.uk) allows you search translated versions of the 'fine rolls' – records of money offered to Henry III for various concessions and favours. British History Online (british-history. ac.uk) also gives access to medieval sources, including charters and monastic records. The Medieval Soldier (medievalsoldier.org) is a database of 220,000 soldiers compiled from muster rolls and records of protections held at TNA, as well as records drawn from French repositories.

People of Medieval Scotland (www.poms.ac.uk) is the result of two major academic studies, and this website features a consolidated database of around 21,000 individuals recorded in documents written between 1093 and 1314. Similarly, the Prosopography of Anglo-Saxon England (pase.ac.uk) is an attempt to record the names of all inhabitants of England from the late sixth to the end of the eleventh centuries, drawing on all kinds of sources. In addition, you can search names recorded in the Domesday Book at opendomesday.org/name/.

Maps

More and more digitised historic maps are pouring online. Some, like tithe maps and their accompanying apportionment data, have more direct genealogical value. TNA's collection can be searched via www.thegenealogist.co.uk/tithe/. The contents of this date from 1837 to the early 1850s, and were a survey of land usage, ownership and occupation in England and Wales. TNA's guide is at: nationalarchives.gov.uk/help-with-your-research/research-guides/tithes/. Welsh researchers can explore Cynefin: A Sense of Place (cynefin.archiveswales.org.uk), a crowdsourcing project which grants us access to 1,200 sheets of Welsh tithe maps, while the accompanying apportionment documents are being transcribed by volunteers. There are other local tithe-map projects too, such as the West Yorkshire Tithe Map Project (tracksintime. wyjs.org.uk).

Away from tithes, the National Library of Scotland gives access to many thousands of maps via maps.nls.uk/. These are free-to-view and include military maps, estate maps, town plans, Ordnance Survey maps and trench maps. Other useful websites include OldMapsOnline (oldmapsonline.org), ScotlandsPlaces (scotlandsplaces.gov.uk), which draws on material from several important national collections, and Vision of Britain (visionofbritain.org.uk). British History Online (british-history. ac.uk/catalogue/maps) hosts historic maps of London and you can read about Griffith's Valuation of Ireland at askaboutireland. ie/griffith-valuation/index.xml – and also see the original valuation maps.

Other gems are Addressing History (addressinghistory. edina.ac.uk), which combines data from post office directories with old maps, and Bomb Sight (bombsight.org), a digital bomb census of the London Blitz.

Newspapers

Newspapers can offer all kinds of information not available

The Times *from the day after D-Day reported that 'great assault going well'. The most important newspaper archive is the British Library's – more and more of which can be accessed via britishnewspaperarchive.co.uk.*

elsewhere. If your ancestor was involved in some newsworthy event, a local civic celebration, a strike or dispute, sporting event or works outing, a strike, a crime, was a witness in a court case or died in circumstances that prompted an inquest, you may find some contemporary reports. Indeed, in some cases the report of an incident is the only evidence that survives. You can search national and regional newspapers for notices of births, marriages or deaths, or more detailed printed obituaries.

Many current newspapers run their own pay-per-view/ subscription archives, but the leading subscription website in the field is the British Newspaper Archive (britishnewspaper archive. co.uk). It offers access to an expanding database of newspapers held at the British Library's newspaper collections. Alongside national British and Irish titles, it has local newspapers from England, Scotland and Wales. Searching is free, but it costs to view the resulting images.

Welsh Newspapers Online (newspapers.library.wales) offers free access to collections of newspapers had at the National Library of Wales. You can search by categories such as family notices and advertisements, browse by exact date, date range or by region/title. It currently boasts 15 million articles and 1.1 million pages.

Another wonderful free resource is the Gazette (www. thegazette.co.uk), offering access to Britain's official public record – the London, Edinburgh and Belfast gazettes. The site has been given a makeover in recent years which enables you to search for specific content such as wills and probate, insolvency and military/civilian awards. A great overseas example is Australia's Trove (trove.nla.gov.au), which offers access to books, images and historic newspapers – which you can search by title, date or region.

Schools
School records not only document your ancestor's education, but

also reveal a great deal about the wider community in which they lived.

Admission registers include names, addresses and dates of pupils, and sometimes other genealogically useful details. Essex Record Office has the admission register of Maldon National School, which besides being a remarkably early example (it starts in 1817) is also unusual in giving the father's occupation. Aberdeenshire Archives looks after an example from Alford Academy, which records child's date of admission to the school, date of birth, name, name of parent/guardian and address.

Meanwhile, log books can contain enlightening references to individual children, as well as bouts of sickness, civil celebrations, parents and more. The Kelso North Pubic School Log Book, dated 14 June 1875 (held by the Scottish Borders Archive and Local History Centre), records the 'very filthy state' of one Isabella Brotherston. Similarly, a page from Tywyn school log book, July 1864 (held in Meirionnydd Record Office, Wales) notes, 'Many of the children were very dirty in this afternoon's school . . .'. The same log book also includes references to use of the 'Welsh Not' or 'Welsh Stick', a punishment system used to dissuade children from speaking Welsh. Meanwhile, the Hebridean Archives holds a log book from the school on the island of St Kilda, which was famously abandoned in 1930. The final entry reads: 'Today very probably ends the school in St Kilda as all the inhabitants intend leaving the island this summer.'

Findmypast has been leading a multi-archive project to digitised school admission registers and log books between 1870 and 1914 (search.findmypast.co.uk/search-world-records/national -school-admission-registers-and-log-books-1870-1914). Findmy past also has some teacher registration records. Ancestry has London School Admissions & Discharges (1840–1911), digitised from the London Metropolitan Archives' school collections – it contains more than 1 million students from 843 different schools.

Some other useful websites include Hidden Lives (hidden

lives.org.uk), which explores the schooling of children in the care of the Children's Society (formerly the Waifs and Strays Society) from 1881. The Workhouse website (workhouses.org.uk) is also helpful in finding out about reform schools.

Some schools have produced their own online archives. Good examples include Radley College Archives (radleyarchives.co.uk), which features registers, staff records, photographs, newsletters and more. Manchester High School for Girls Archive (www.mhsg archive.org) allows you to explore letters, governors' minutes, newspaper cuttings, programmes, school magazines and reports.

Similarly, if you are tracing an ancestor's university career, it's well worth seeing if the university archives are available online – more and more are. Via the University of Glasgow website (universitystory.gla.ac.uk), for example, you can browse records of 19,050 graduates of the University from its foundation in 1451 until 1914.

Taxation and Valuation

Taxation records can function as pre-census surveys of the population, and, in Ireland in particular, are often the only potential source for genealogists. The Hearth Tax (hearthtax. org.uk), for example, was levied between 1662 and 1689 on each householder according to the number of hearths in his or her dwelling. Therefore, it can represent a kind of census, recording the head-of-household of each property. Another important site is ScotlandsPlaces (scotlandsplaces.gov.uk) which has an army of volunteers transcribing all sorts of data, including various tax rolls – such as servant tax rolls, the farm horse tax and poll tax records from the 1690s.

The aforementioned Griffith's Valuation of Ireland (askaboutireland.ie/griffith-valuation/index.xml) was a detailed survey of every taxable piece of agricultural or built property between the years 1847 and 1864. The valuation books recorded

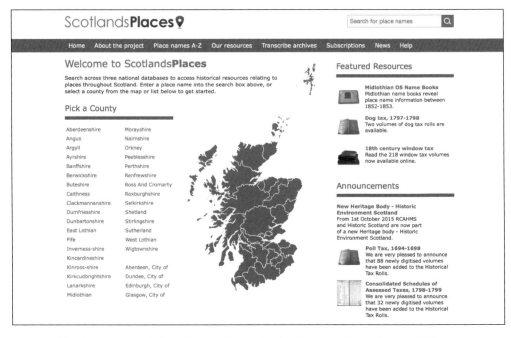

Two important websites for taxation and valuation records are ScotlandsPlaces (scotlandsplaces.gov.uk) and Griffith's Valuation of Ireland (askaboutireland. ie/griffith-valuation/index.xml), a detailed survey of every taxable piece of agricultural or built property between the years 1847 and 1864.

the names of occupiers and landowners, and the amount and value of the property held. Ancestry's collections include London Land Tax Records (1692–1932), Findmypast has Rate Books, which list the owners/occupiers of properties on which rates were paid. Similarly, an important source for Scottish researchers is the Valuation Rolls, available via ScotlandsPeople. Following an Act of 1854 these were compiled listing every house or piece of ground in Scotland, along with the names/designations of proprietor, tenant and occupier. Finally, the wonderful Building History has a page focussing on property taxation: building history.org/taxation.shtml.

INDEX

Index

Index

medicine, 143
medieval sources, 174
Medway, 13
Meirionnydd Record Office, 57, 178
memorial plaque, 114
memory, 9
merchant seaman, 142
message boards, 26
Methodism, 77, 78, 85
migration, 100
Militia Act, 121
militia records, 43, 118, 121
millers, 140
miners, 133, 140
Ministry of Defence, 117, 118
Modern Records Centre, 139
monumental inscriptions, 71

names, 1
Napoleonic Wars, 43
The National Archives, 20, 24, 26, 44, 52,
    80, 87, 97, 102, 104, 107, 116, 121, 135,
    138, 150, 154, 159, 169, 173
national archives and libraries, 20
National Archives of Australia, 106
National Archives of Ireland, 20, 50, 95,
    98, 135
National Archives of Scotland, 20
National Army Museum, 128
National Burial Index, 63
National Coal Mining Museum, 24
National Library of Ireland, 20, 61, 81
National Library of Scotland, 20, 175
National Library of Wales, 20, 74, 89, 98,
    135, 155, 159, 177
National Maritime Museum, 128
National Probate Index, 92
National Records of Scotland, 41, 61, 90,
    92, 135, 151, 154, 159, 169, 172, 173
naturalisation records, 83, 103
Naval History, 128
Navy Lists, 118
navy research, 116
Nelson, 116
New Poor Law, 69
New Zealand, 105
newsgroups, 26
newspapers, 23, 34, 175
Nonconformity, 77
North East Inheritance Database, 98

North Riding Archives, 16
North Yorkshire County Record Office,
    16, 123
note taking, 5
Nottingham, 74

occupations, 131
Old Bailey, 108, 153, 155
Old Parish Registers, 54, 60
Online Parish Clerks, 64
overseers accounts, 68, 71

parish chest records, 66
parish church, 15
parish registers, 54
    keeping registers, 56
Parish Register Society, 63
parishes, 12, 14, 55
passenger lists, 105
Paton, Chris, 4
paupers, 151
Peninsular Roll Call, 128
Phillimore, 63
policing, 141
Poll Books, 42, 171
Poor Law, 31, 68, 106, 149, 150, 157
pre-census records, 42
prerogative courts, 92
Presbyterians, 78, 86
Prince of Wales's Own Regiment of
    Yorkshire, 123
prisons, 46, 155, 170
probate, 89
Probate Search, 93
professional researchers, 27
Protestation Returns, 1642, 42
province, 17
Public Record Office of Northern Ireland,
    20, 51, 81, 95, 98, 135, 169, 172
publicans, 147

Quaker marriages, 32
Quakers, 78, 87
Queen's Royal Surrey Regiment, 123

Radley College Archives, 179
rail workers, 141
Rate Books, 181
ratings records, 116
regimental archives, 121

185